GOVERNMENT PROCEDURES AND OPERATIONS

IRS BUDGETS

EFFECTS AND RESPONSE TO CONSTRAINTS AND UNCERTAINTY

GOVERNMENT PROCEDURES AND OPERATIONS

Additional books in this series can be found on Nova's website under the Series tab.

Additional e-books in this series can be found on Nova's website under the e-book tab.

GOVERNMENT PROCEDURES AND OPERATIONS

IRS BUDGETS

EFFECTS AND RESPONSE TO CONSTRAINTS AND UNCERTAINTY

NICOLAS B. CUNNINGHAM
EDITOR

nova publishers
New York

Library of Congress Cataloging-in-Publication Data

ISBN: 978-1-63484-466-6

Published by Nova Science Publishers, Inc. † New York

CONTENTS

Preface		**vii**
Chapter 1	IRS 2016 Budget: IRS Is Scaling Back Activities and Using Budget Flexibilities to Absorb Funding Cuts *United States Government Accountability Office*	**1**
Chapter 2	IRS 2015 Budget: Long-Term Strategy and Return on Investment Data Needed to Better Manage Budget Uncertainty and Set Priorities *United States Government Accountability Office*	**57**
Index		**103**

PREFACE

The financing of the federal government depends largely upon Internal Revenue Service's (IRS) ability to collect taxes, including providing taxpayer services that make voluntary compliance easier and enforcing tax laws to ensure compliance with tax responsibilities. This book analyzes select IRS business units' budget and staffing; describes how IRS is managing in a constrained budget environment; assesses key data for information technology (IT) investments; and describes IRS progress in implementing selected United States Government Accountability Office (GAO) open recommendations. Furthermore, the book assesses IRS's strategy to address budget cuts and use of return on investment (ROI) analysis.

In: IRS Budgets
Editor: Nicolas B. Cunningham
ISBN: 978-1-63484-466-6

Chapter 1

IRS 2016 BUDGET: IRS IS SCALING BACK ACTIVITIES AND USING BUDGET FLEXIBILITIES TO ABSORB FUNDING CUTS*

United States Government Accountability Office

WHY GAO DID THIS STUDY

The financing of the federal government depends largely upon IRS's ability to collect taxes, including providing taxpayer services that make voluntary compliance easier and enforcing tax laws to ensure compliance with tax responsibilities. For fiscal year 2016, the President requested $12.9 billion in appropriations for IRS; the request is almost $2 billion (18 percent) more than IRS's fiscal year 2015 appropriation.

Because of the size of IRS's budget and the importance of its service and compliance programs for all taxpayers, GAO was asked to review the fiscal year 2016 budget request for IRS and the effects of recent budget constraints. In February 2015, GAO reported interim information on IRS's budget. This report (1) analyzes select IRS business units' budget and staffing; (2) describes how IRS is managing in a constrained budget environment; (3) assesses key data for IT investments; and (4) describes IRS progress in implementing selected GAO open recommendations. To conduct this work, GAO reviewed

* This is an edited, reformatted and augmented version of a United States Government Accountability Office publication, No. GAO-15-624, dated June 2015.

the fiscal year 2016 CJ, IRS and Office of Management and Budget guidance, and IRS data from fiscal years 2010 to 2014, and interviewed IRS officials.

What GAO Recommends

GAO recommends that IRS implement controls to ensure that information reported on major IT investments is accurate, define key terms in the CJ, and continue implementing previous recommendations. IRS agreed with the recommendations.

What GAO Found

Business unit trends. Internal Revenue Service (IRS) total appropriations declined from a high of $12.1 billion in fiscal year 2010 to $11.3 billion in fiscal year 2014, a reduction of about 7 percent. GAO selected business units with large declines in obligations—both dollar amount and percent—from fiscal year 2010 to fiscal year 2014, the most current spending data available. To absorb budget cuts, the business units GAO reviewed—Human Capital Office, Office of Chief Counsel, and Small Business/Self-Employed Division—each reduced staff (full-time equivalents or FTEs) by 16 to 30 percent. According to officials, they also prioritized legally required programs, such as tax litigation, and reduced some programs or services, such as limiting non-filer investigations, postponing software acquisitions, and delaying approximately 24,000 employee background reinvestigations. Such scaled back activities potentially reduce program effectiveness or increase risk to IRS and the federal government.

Budget environment. IRS's budget decreased by an additional $346 million from fiscal year 2014 to fiscal year 2015. IRS used its flexibility to absorb this reduction by allocating user fee revenue, which comprised 3.4 percent of its budget, or $416 million, in fiscal year 2014. Additionally, to increase agency-wide coordination of budget decisions, IRS formed a new office and committee to inform budget formulation and execution decisions.

Information technology data. IRS requested $3.2 billion for information technology (IT) investments. This accounted for 23 percent of IRS's budget request for fiscal year 2016. However, IRS provided inaccurate data on actual obligations to date for major IT investments in its congressional justification

(CJ) for fiscal year 2016. As a result, Congress does not have accurate, reliable, and complete data on IT investments to inform its budget decisions or aid in its oversight. Additionally, IRS did not use standard definitions for "life-cycle cost" and "projected useful life of the current asset" or explain the terms in a way that could be understood and used.

Change in Full-Time Equivalents at Selected Business Units, Fiscal Years 2010-2014

Business unit	Fiscal year 2014 FTEs	Change in FTEs from fiscal year 2010 to 2014	Percent change in FTEs from fiscal year 2010 to 2014
Human Capital Office	1,205	-506	-29.6%
Office of Chief Counsel	2,101	-402	-16.1%
Small Business/Self-Employed	21,681	-5,417	-20.0%

Source: GAO analysis of IRS data. | GAO-15-624

Open GAO recommendations. Eighty-eight recommendations and eight matters for congressional consideration could have financial implications if implemented. IRS made progress implementing many recommendations, including two particularly important ones. First, IRS has begun to estimate return on investment for specific compliance projects within its correspondence exam program. Second, IRS's updated cost estimate for the Patient Protection and Affordable Care Act improved from previous versions and met or substantially met the criteria in three of four overall categories, but is still not reliable because it only partially met the criteria in the overall credibility category.

ABBREVIATIONS

Counsel	Office of Chief Counsel
CJ	congressional justification
FTE	full-time equivalent
HCO	Human Capital Office

IRS	Internal Revenue Service
IT	information technology
OMB	Office of Management and Budget
PPAC	Planning, Programming, and Audit Coordination
PPACA	Patient Protection and Affordable Care Act
ROI	return on investment
SB/SE	Small Business Self-Employed Division

* * *

June 24, 2015

The Honorable John Boozman
Chairman
The Honorable Chris Coons
Ranking Member
Subcommittee on Financial Services
and General Government
Committee on Appropriations
United States Senate

The Honorable Charles Boustany, Jr.
Chairman
Subcommittee on Human Resources
Committee on Ways and Means
House of Representatives

The Honorable Peter Roskam
Chairman

The Honorable John Lewis
Ranking Member
Subcommittee on Oversight
Committee on Ways and Means
House of Representatives

The financing of the federal government depends largely upon the Internal Revenue Service (IRS), which collected 93 percent of federal receipts in fiscal year 2014. IRS's mission is to provide taxpayers top-quality services by helping them understand and meet their tax responsibilities and to enforce the law with integrity and fairness to all. The President proposes a budget that reflects how IRS plans to use its resources to accomplish these tasks, while also continuing to invest in modernizing its information systems, among other things. In February 2015, we reported that IRS's fiscal year 2015 appropriations ($10.9 billion) and staffing levels (81,279 full-time equivalents, or FTEs) continue a decline that has occurred over several years and are now below fiscal year 2009 levels.[1] Since fiscal year 2010, IRS's annual appropriations have declined by $1.2 billion (9.9 percent), and staffing has declined by about 13,000 FTEs (14.1 percent).[2] For fiscal year 2016, the President requested $12.9 billion in appropriations for IRS to support 90,524 FTEs. The President's Budget request is almost $2 billion (18 percent) and about 9,200 FTEs (11 percent) more than the fiscal year 2015 appropriation.

Because of the size of IRS's budget and the importance of its service and compliance programs for taxpayers, you asked us to review its fiscal year 2016 budget request and the effects of recent budget constraints. In this report we (1) analyze IRS's business units' budgets for fiscal years 2010 through 2014 and for selected units, describe staffing and programs changes; (2) describe how IRS plans to absorb fiscal year 2015 budget cuts and the steps IRS has taken to improve agency-wide coordination on budget decisions; (3) summarize and assess key performance information for IRS's major information technology (IT) investments; and (4) describe our open recommendations and prior work that, if implemented, could improve IRS operations or have a financial impact or that relate to legislative proposals.

We selected three business units or fund centers—Human Capital Office (HCO), Office of Chief Counsel (Counsel), and Small Business/SelfEmployed Division (SB/SE)—to determine how they managed their budget and to identify examples of the effects of budget reductions. We selected business units with large declines in obligations—both dollar amount and percent—from fiscal year 2010 to fiscal year 2014, the most current spending data available. One business unit was selected from each category of fund center: support (HCO), functional (Counsel), and operating (SB/SE). We also analyzed IRS's Financial Management Codes Handbooks and conducted interviews and reviewed documentation from Corporate Budget and each of the selected business units. In addition, we reviewed documentation about IRS's budget execution process and IRS's fiscal year 2016 congressional justification (CJ).

To examine planned reductions for 2015, we reviewed IRS documents on its proposed fiscal year 2015 budget savings and reductions. To describe IRS's user fee funding, we reviewed IRS's authority to collect and spend user fees, and the President's Budget requests from fiscal years 2013 through 2016. To describe efforts to increase coordination, we reviewed IRS documents on the Program and Budget Advisory Committee and the Planning, Programming, and Audit Coordination (PPAC) office. In addition, we interviewed IRS officials in Corporate Budget.

We analyzed reported cost and schedule data for major IT investments and interviewed agency officials to assess the accuracy of these data and the procedures used to report information to Congress. We compared key performance data reported in the fiscal year 2015 and 2016 CJs to other IRS data and assessed the extent to which IRS reporting complied with Office of Management and Budget (OMB) guidance and GAO internal control standards.[3]

We interviewed IRS officials and analyzed documentation on the status of open recommendations to determine if the recommendations were implemented, including interviewing IRS officials about calculating and using return on investment (ROI) data to inform resource allocation decisions. We also compared IRS's current Patient Protection and Affordable Care Act (PPACA)[4] cost estimate (version 3) to the characteristics of a high-quality cost estimate as identified in the GAO Cost Guide.[5]

As applicable for each objective, we interviewed IRS officials and reviewed data collection procedures and determined that the data used in this report were sufficiently reliable for our purposes. We conducted this performance audit from December 2014 to June 2015 in accordance with generally accepted government auditing standards. Those standards require that we plan and perform the audit to obtain sufficient, appropriate evidence to provide a reasonable basis for our findings and conclusions based on our audit objectives. We believe that the evidence obtained provides a reasonable basis for our findings and conclusions based on our audit objectives.

BACKGROUND

IRS Budget Formulation and Execution Structures

IRS formulates its budget at three levels: (1) appropriation account, (2) budget activity, and (3) program activity. IRS requests funding by appropriation accounts, which align broadly with its strategic goals, which are to (1) deliver high quality and timely service to reduce taxpayer burden and encourage voluntary compliance; and (2) effectively enforce the law to ensure compliance with tax responsibilities and combat fraud. IRS's CJ presents funding and FTE information at the appropriation account and budget activity levels. In addition, it provides descriptions of program activities within each budget activity. IRS has four appropriation accounts (fiscal year 2015 appropriation listed in parentheses):[6]

- **Enforcement** ($4.86 billion): Funds activities such as determining and collecting owed taxes, providing legal and litigation support, and conducting criminal investigations.
- **Operations Support** ($3.64 billion): Funds activities including rent and facilities expenses, IRS-wide administration activities, and IT maintenance and security.
- **Taxpayer Services** ($2.16 billion): Funds taxpayer service activities and programs, including pre-filing assistance and education, filing and account services, and taxpayer advocacy services.
- **Business Systems Modernization** ($290 million): Funds the planning and capital asset acquisition of IT to modernize IRS business systems.

Budget activities divide appropriation accounts into additional functions. For example, the Enforcement appropriation is broken into three budget activities: Investigations, Exam and Collections, and Regulatory. Each budget activity, in turn, has multiple program activities. For example, Exam and Collections has 20 program activities, such as Tax Reporting Compliance – Field Exam; Earned Income Tax Credit Management and Administration; and Whistleblower Office. In addition to program activities, the lower levels of the budget formulation and budget execution structures include business units and other areas of interest, which are not discrete categories. For example, Wage and Investment is one division within IRS and can be referred to as a business unit, while identity theft would be considered an area of interest that crosses divisions within IRS.

IRS's appropriation accounts align with its organizational structure at the highest level. For example, IRS has an Operations Support appropriation account and an Operations Support commissioner-level organization. In addition, IRS's organizational structure tracks roughly to its budget execution structure, which is made up of three types of fund centers: (1) support, (2) functional, and (3) operating. IRS executes its budget across 18 fund centers, which manage and distribute funds.

Budget Flexibility

IRS has some flexibility in how it allocates its resources. IRS may shift resources among program activities (activities within a budget activity). For example, IRS could shift resources among any of the 20 program activities within the Exam and Collection budget activity without congressional approval or notification. Additionally, IRS may reprogram funds among budget activities within certain limits.[7]

While IRS cannot transfer resources from one appropriation account to another without specific statutory authority to do so, the agency still has some flexibility because fund centers may receive funds from more than one appropriation account.[8] Over half of IRS fund centers or business units receive funding and obligate funds from multiple appropriation accounts. IRS management allocates funds to each business unit (subject to transfer and reprogramming limitations) and has more flexibility when there are multiple accounts from which it may fund a business unit.

IRS also has flexibility in how it allocates user fees because it determines the amount of funds transferred to each appropriation account.[9] In fiscal year 2014, IRS transferred $416 million in user fee funds to its appropriations accounts to be spent. IRS collects user fees for various activities such as assisting taxpayers in complying with their tax liabilities, clarifying the application of the tax code to particular circumstances, and ensuring the quality of paid preparers of tax returns.

Information Technology

IT comprises a significant portion of IRS's budget and plays a critical role in enabling IRS to carry out its mission and responsibilities. The fiscal year 2015 appropriation includes about $2.5 billion for IT investments; this represents over 20 percent of the total IRS budget. IRS relies on information systems to process tax returns, account for tax revenues collected, send bills for taxes owed, issue refunds, assist in the selection of tax returns for audit, and provide telecommunications services for all business activities, including the taxpayer toll-free access to tax information, among other things.

IT investments are funded through both the Operations Support and the Business Systems Modernization appropriation accounts as well as through user fees. The President's fiscal year 2016 budget request includes $3.24 billion for IRS IT investments. Of that amount, $2.26 billion is for 20 major IT investments.[10] These major IT investments are subject to additional reporting requirements.

FUNDING DECLINED FOR MOST IRS BUSINESS UNITS AND TRADEOFFS TO MANAGE REDUCTIONS MAY AFFECT SOME PROGRAMS' EFFECTIVENESS AND INCREASE RISK

Fifteen of Eighteen Business Units Decreased Spending

IRS's total appropriations declined from a high of $12.1 billion in fiscal year 2010 to $11.3 billion in fiscal year 2014, a reduction of about 7 percent.[11] Reflecting IRS's overall budget decline, spending fell in 15 of the 18 fund centers or business units from fiscal year 2010 to fiscal year 2014, and spending in 9 fund centers declined 10 percent or more.[12] For example, SB/SE, which was the largest business unit in fiscal year 2010, experienced a 14 percent decrease in obligations—from $2.6 billion to $2.3 billion—from fiscal year 2010 to fiscal year 2014. Over half of IRS fund centers or business units receive appropriations from multiple accounts. As shown in figure 1, of the 18 fund centers, 11 obligate funds from two or more of IRS's four appropriation accounts.[13] In addition, 7 fund centers obligate funds from only one account and 5 of those 7 serve in an operational support capacity, such as Agency Wide Shared Services, HCO, and Chief Financial Officer. Of the 9 fund centers that experienced a decline in obligations of at least 10 percent, 5 receive funding from only one appropriation account. Business units that receive funds from more than one appropriation account may have increased flexibility because IRS can balance reductions in one account with resources from another account, provided that any shifts in funding do not violate appropriation, transfer or reprogramming restrictions.

See Appendix II for additional information regarding Figure 1.

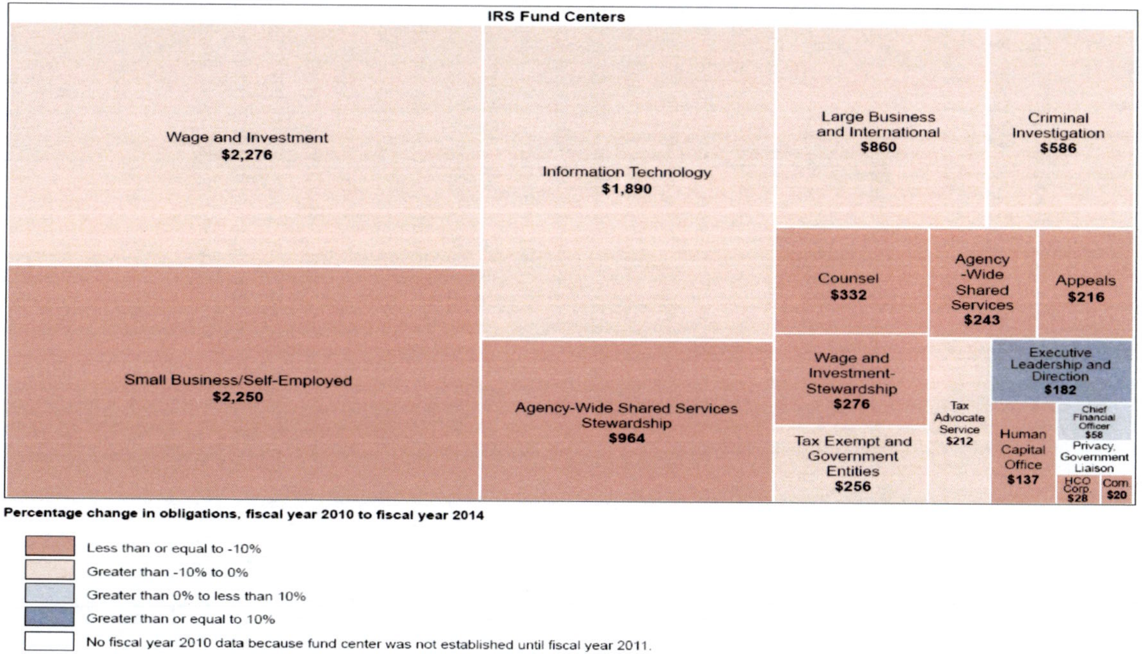

Notes: Numbers may not add due to rounding.

We did not include in our analysis the Centralized Payments fund center, which is for unemployment and worker's compensation.

This figure does not include obligations less than $1 million. In fiscal year 2014, 4 fund centers obligated less than $1 million from additional accounts: Counsel ($222,000 from Operations Support); Communications & Liaison ($92,000 from Taxpayer Services and $6,000 from Enforcement); Criminal Investigations ($38,000 from Operations Support); and Privacy, Governmental Liaison and Disclosure ($29,000 from Enforcement).

Figure 1. Fiscal Year 2014 Obligations by Fund Center and Percentage Change from Fiscal Year 2010.

Selected Business Units Scaled Back Activities, Potentially Reducing Program Effectiveness or Increasing Risk to IRS and the Federal Government

Each business unit we examined—HCO, Office of Chief Counsel, and SB/SE—took actions to absorb budget reductions. One common element among each of the business units examined is that they spend 80 percent or more of their funds on labor. When IRS receives its budget, the Corporate Budget Office coordinates with business units to ensure that each business unit has sufficient funding to support FTEs already onboard. The review of FTEs aligns anticipated salary and benefit costs to available appropriated funding for each business unit. As seen in Table 1, from fiscal year 2010 to fiscal year 2014, FTEs declined through attrition in each of the business units examined.

Table 1. Change in Full-Time Equivalents (FTEs) from Fiscal Year 2010 through Fiscal Year 2014 for Selected Business Units

Business Unit	Fiscal year 2014 FTEs	Change in FTEs from fiscal year 2010 to 2014 (number)	Change in FTEs from fiscal year 2010 to 2014 (percent)
Human Capital Office	1,205	-506	-29.6%
Office of Chief Counsel	2,101	-402	-16.1%
Small Business/Self-Employed	21,681	-5,417	-20.0%

Source: GAO analysis of IRS data. | GAO-15-624

Because labor comprises the majority of these business units' expenses, unit managers are limited in how they implement budget cuts. According to business unit officials, budget reductions were often implemented by decreasing the amount or type of activity performed. One key factor that influenced business units' decisions about how to prioritize activities was whether the activity was statutorily mandated. According to IRS officials, statutorily mandated activities—such as tax litigation in the Office of Chief Counsel—remained a priority.

Examples of Programs and Services Reduced or Eliminated

- **Non-filer investigations.** SB/SE significantly reduced the individual and business non-filer cases it pursues. IRS detects taxpayers that failed to file—non-filers—by matching third party information with tax returns for individuals, and relying on open filing requirements and third party information for businesses. In tax year 2010, IRS started 3.5 million individual non-filer cases and 4.3 million business non-filer cases. In tax year 2014 non-filer cases dropped to 2.0 million for individuals and 1.8 million for businesses, a reduction of 43 percent and 58 percent, respectively. According to SB/SE officials, detecting and pursuing non-filers is not mandatory. By not pursing non-filers, however, IRS misses the opportunity to bring a noncompliant taxpayer into the tax system, and the government could forego potential revenue from taxes, penalties and interest payments.

- **Private letter rulings.** The Office of Chief Counsel limited the number and scope of private letter rulings—a written statement issued by IRS at the request of a taxpayer that interprets and applies tax laws to the taxpayer's represented set of facts. Private letter rulings decreased by 30 percent—from 935 to 651—from fiscal year 2010 through 2014. The drop in private letter rulings means that fewer taxpayers receive a ruling prior to filing, causing uncertainty for them and the tax community. According to Counsel officials, one benefit of the private letter rulings is that they can alert IRS attorneys to nascent tax issues. Private letter rulings are not mandatory and IRS charges a user fee for the service to offset the cost of the service. However, since there are a limited number of FTEs, IRS decided to scale back work in the area in order to shift those FTEs to other activities, such as issuing regulations and public guidance.
- **Bankruptcy program.** According to Counsel officials, a bankruptcy program supported by approximately 30 FTEs was eliminated. IRS attorneys supporting the program were appointed as Special Assistant United States Attorneys to represent IRS in bankruptcy court instead of Department of Justice attorneys. The program was identified as low priority because it was not required by statute.

Examples of Deferred Programs or Acquisitions

- **Software acquisitions.** According to officials in the Office of the Chief Counsel, the limited budget for litigation-related information technology has prevented Counsel from acquiring modern, industry standard electronic discovery software. Such software is used to capture and preserve documents for the discovery phase of tax and other litigation. According to Counsel officials, the outcome of tax litigation cases has been impacted because IRS does not have the software. For example, parties to a lawsuit frequently request emails and other computer files related to a particular topic or keywords, and the software thoroughly and efficiently identifies the files, minimizing the need for time-intensive manual review of the files. IRS was recently sanctioned in court and ordered to reimburse a plaintiff $12,500 for the cost of depositions because it did not have the technical capability to produce appropriate documents for discovery. This issue has been raised with IRS management through the Enterprise Risk Management and budget processes. Counsel officials stated that IRS has funded other high-priority IT systems, but that there has not been sufficient funding to acquire e-discovery software or support an effective e-discovery function. IRS estimates the cost of the software is $10 million.

- **Background reinvestigations.** IRS has postponed reinvestigations for moderate risk employees since fiscal year 2013. Almost half of IRS's FTEs, approximately 38,000 employees, are identified as moderate risk, and 24,000 reinvestigations have been postponed. In November 2011, the Office of Personnel Management amended its regulations to direct that federal employees occupying positions of public trust (those designated as high or moderate risk) undergo a background reinvestigation every 5 years.[14] Periodic reinvestigations allow agencies to determine if employees are still suitable for U.S. government employment, or still eligible to hold a sensitive position. IRS completed reinvestigations in fiscal year 2012 at a cost of approximately $3.9 million. For fiscal year 2016, the President's Budget requests $3.5 million and 11 FTEs for IRS to implement federal investigative standards, which includes reinvestigations of employees.

IRS Is Using Its Budgeting Flexibility and Taking Steps to Improve Agency-Wide Coordination of Budget Decisions

IRS Has Flexibility in Spending User Fee Revenue

In fiscal year 2015, IRS plans to allocate less user fee revenue to the taxpayer services account than in previous years ($49 million, compared to around $180 million in fiscal years 2012, 2013, and 2014). IRS plans to allocate a larger amount to the operations support account ($411 million, compared to $132 million, $183 million, and $218 million in fiscal years 2012, 2013, and 2014, respectively). According to IRS officials, management decided to allocate more user fee funds to operations support in fiscal year 2015, in part because that year's appropriation for operations support was $161 million (4.2 percent) less than fiscal year 2014, while taxpayer services was not reduced during that time frame. According to IRS officials, user fee revenue allocated to operations support will be used to meet requirements to implement PPACA and fund investment in the design, development, and deployment of mainframe and server investments which can help IRS better respond to taxpayers. IRS officials said that user fees allocated to operations support reduce system downtime, which positively affects IRS's ability to respond to taxpayers, process returns, collect revenue and issue refunds.

IRS User Fees The Secretary of the Treasury may establish new fees or raise existing fees for services provided by IRS to increase receipts, where such fees are authorized by another law, and may spend the new or increased fee receipts to supplement appropriations made available to IRS appropriations accounts. See GAO-12-193 for additional information about IRS user fees.

Source: Pub. L. No. 103-329, § 3 and GAO. | GAO-15-624

Although IRS services and operations are primarily funded through annual appropriations, IRS has the flexibility to supplement its appropriations with other resources, such as user fees. IRS deposits user fees that it is authorized to retain into its Miscellaneous Retained Fees Fund before transferring funds to an appropriation account to be spent. In fiscal year 2014, $677 million was available in the account. IRS transferred $416 million of that money to its appropriation accounts which accounted for 3.4 percent of IRS's total available resources. Remaining funds are carried over to the next fiscal year. Table 2 shows user fee funds transferred to IRS's appropriation accounts during recent fiscal years. For fiscal year 2015, IRS plans to transfer a total of $481 million.

Table 2. IRS User Fee Transfers to Appropriation Accounts (Dollars in Millions)

Appropriation account	Fiscal year					
	2011	2012	2013	2014	2015 (planned)	2016 (estimated)
Taxpayer Services	$129	$174	$190	$183	$49	$56
Operations Support	79	132	183	218	411	379
Business Systems Modernization	89	-	-	-	-	-
Enforcement	13	20	20	15	21	16
Total transferred	$310	$326	$394	$416	$481	$451

Source: President's Budget from fiscal year 2013 through 2016 and IRS data. | GAO-15-624

Note: Some numbers do not add due to rounding.

IRS Planning Efforts Informed the Management of $346 Million in Budget Reductions

IRS managed reductions by strictly limiting hiring, overtime, and overhead costs. The reductions were informed by a December 2014 planning exercise. In this exercise, IRS prepared for how it would absorb a hypothetical 5 percent budget reduction. Business unit managers identified funding requirements for current activities and categorized programs as high, medium, or low priority, including how the proposed reduction would affect program spending and FTE counts. Business unit officials identified and documented legally or contractually required activities and also identified potential risks and the potential performance impact of cutting or not funding each activity. Ultimately, IRS's budget decreased $346 million from fiscal year 2014 to fiscal year 2015, a 3.1 percent decline. IRS considered furloughing employees for up to 2 days in fiscal year 2015 to help absorb the budget cuts; it since determined that furlough days will not be necessary because it is able to absorb the reductions in other areas.

Following the planning exercise, in January 2015, IRS identified the following actions to absorb this budget reduction.

- **External hiring freeze:** IRS plans to replace few employees who leave the agency. In an agency with over 80,000 FTEs, all requests for external hiring in fiscal year 2015 must be approved by a direct report to the Commissioner. Specifically, requests for new hires are reviewed by the Deputy Commissioner for Operations Support, Deputy Commissioner for Services and Enforcement, and in certain cases, the Chief of Staff.

- **Internal hiring restrictions:** New policies require that resources be available to cover both current year and annualized future costs for any internal hiring, permanent promotions, or reassignments. These policies ensure that employee transfers are consistent with the workflow needs of the agency.
- **Overtime restrictions:** Overtime was eliminated except for a small amount to support the tax filing season or for mission critical needs. IRS uses overtime frequently during the tax filing season to process tax returns and provide taxpayers service, such as by telephone or at assistance centers. All overtime requests were to be approved by the Deputy Commissioners or the Chief of Staff to the Commissioner. According to IRS officials, limitations on overtime are estimated to save approximately $75 million.
- **Overhead cost reductions:** Spending on travel and training, contracts, and supplies and printing is restricted and business unit heads are required to review the priorities for contract spending and identify lower cost alternatives.

IRS Is Working to Increase Agency-Wide Coordination in Budget Decisions in Response to Constrained Budget Environment

Recently, IRS launched two efforts to increase management coordination in budget formulation and execution decisions. In one effort, IRS established the Program and Budget Advisory Committee to help it improve its process for determining agency-wide priorities and for allocating resources to fund those priorities. According to IRS officials, this committee was formed in October 2014. It is intended to prevent resources from being allocated on a first come, first served basis or on some other arbitrary method. Members of the committee include executives from Strategy and Finance, Budget Execution, Systems and Analysis, and Corporate Budget; the Commissioner and Deputy Commissioners have decision-making authority. According to IRS, the committee will be responsible for overseeing and reviewing IRS's budget execution and making recommendations on all matters relating to its financial operations. These include making recommendations for allocating funds, prioritizing mission critical needs, and assessing and reporting risk with regard to expending resources. IRS expects the outcomes to include a detailed decision-making process for prioritizing IRS-wide requirements that are aligned with its strategy and resource needs, open communication and transparency, and identification of risk and requirements in excess of available funds.

In another effort, responding in part to our June 2014 recommendation,[15] IRS established the Planning, Programming, and Audit Coordination (PPAC) office[16] in 2014 to improve coordination of (1) current and completed audits of IRS activities and (2) resource decision making and strategic planning. According to IRS, PPAC is to facilitate coordination among business units and operating divisions to improve resource allocation and planning as part of the budget formulation process. PPAC is to drive long-term planning for resource allocation to be seen first in the fiscal year 2017 budget. As envisioned, the new strategic approach is to include consideration of short-term trade-offs with long-term investments along with post-evaluation of investments.

IRS Reported on Major IT Investments in Its Fiscal Year 2016 Congressional Justification, but Some Information Was Inaccurate or Unclear

IRS Provided Inaccurate Data to the Congress

In its fiscal year 2016 CJ, IRS provided detailed information about its major IT investments, as it did in the 2014 and 2015 CJs; however, the information provided on actual obligations to date was inaccurate, due to potential deficiencies in some internal controls over the preparation of the CJ. IT is a significant portion—about 23 percent—of the total IRS budget request for fiscal year 2016. The request includes approximately $2.26 billion to fund 20 major IT investments and approximately $976 million for other IT investments. In the fiscal year 2016 CJ, IRS defines "actual obligations to date" as the actual obligations through fiscal year 2014 specific to each asset.[17] However, despite this definition, the numbers reported for most investments only include obligations through fiscal year 2013. Because the CJ reports inaccurate information about amounts obligated to date for most of the 20 listed major IT investments, Congress does not have accurate, reliable, and current data to inform its budget decisions or aid in its oversight.

IRS increased the amount of information it reported on major IT investments in recent years' CJs, and the fiscal year 2015 and 2016 CJs included information under the label "actual obligations to date" for each investment. Beginning with the fiscal year 2014 CJ, IRS reported detailed and precise quantitative and qualitative information on the cost and duration of its major IT investments. Information reported included life-cycle costs, projected useful life of the current asset, and anticipated benefits for each investment. In the fiscal year 2015 CJ, IRS added information on actual obligations to date for each of the major IT investments listed in the CJ. IRS provided this additional information in response to a recommendation we made in September 2013 for all major IT investments.[18]

IRS reported inaccurate information on actual obligations to date for many of the major IT investments in the fiscal year 2016 CJ. The CJ states that these amounts represent obligations through fiscal year 2014. However, for all of the major IT investments listed in the CJ, with the exception of one newly added major investment, the amounts reported for actual obligations to date through fiscal year 2014 were the same as the amounts reported in the previous year's CJ as actual obligations through fiscal year 2013. Data obtained separately from IRS show that amounts were obligated for all of these investments in fiscal year 2014, which indicates that the data were not updated in the CJ.

Officials in IRS's Corporate Budget office stated that the data may not have been updated since they used last year's information as a starting point in preparing the fiscal year 2016 CJ. According to the officials, staff in the Information Technology office prepare this section of the CJ and send it to Corporate Budget for inclusion in the final submission. Corporate Budget officials relied on data provided by the Information Technology staff without using any internal control procedure, such as checking the data against a reliable source, to confirm that these data were correct before including them in the CJ.

Standards for Internal Control in the Federal Government calls for agencies to ensure that ongoing monitoring occurs during the course of normal operations. Monitoring should be performed continually and be ingrained in the agency's operations; it includes regular management and supervisory activities, comparisons, reconciliations, and other actions people take in performing their duties.[19] Without such controls, IRS risks continued errors in the information on IT investments reported in its CJ. Such errors could negatively affect Congress' ability to obtain accurate information on major IT investments needed to inform future budget decisions and oversight.

Some IT Investment Information Was Unclear Because IRS Did Not Use Standard Definitions

IRS reported information on "life-cycle cost" and "projected useful life of the current asset" for each major IT investment in the fiscal year 2016 CJ, but did not use standard definitions for these terms or define or explain the terms in such a way that they could be understood and used. Agencies are required to use standard terms established by the Comptroller General, in consultation with OMB, in providing fiscal, budget, and program information to Congress.[20] The Comptroller General has established the following definition of life-cycle cost: "The overall estimated cost, both government and contractor, for a particular program alternative over the time period corresponding to the life of the program, including direct and indirect initial costs plus any periodic or continuing costs of operation and maintenance."[21] OMB's Capital Programming Guide applies this definition to capital assets: "The cost of a capital asset is its full life-cycle cost, including all direct and indirect costs for planning, procurement (purchase price and all other costs incurred to bring it to a form and location suitable for its intended use), operations and maintenance (including service contracts), and disposal."[22]

IRS did not report data that are consistent with the required definition of "life-cycle cost" or offer an alternative definition. IRS Information Technology officials told us that the reported amounts represent estimates of full life-cycle costs for some major IT investments. For other investments, these amounts represent estimated costs for the current fiscal year and 2 future fiscal years. According to IRS officials responsible for preparing this portion of the CJ, they did not consider how long the investment was expected to last when deciding which estimates to report. Instead, they reported full life-cycle cost estimates when such estimates were available. When such estimates were not available, the officials reported 3-year estimates. However, the CJ identifies all investments' reported life-cycle costs as representing full life-cycle costs.

In addition, IRS did not explain the meaning of the term "projected useful life of the current asset" in the CJ. In the Financial Services and General Government Appropriations Act, 2015, Congress directed IRS to include in its fiscal year 2016 CJ a summary of cost and schedule performance information for its major IT systems. In order for this performance information to be useful to Congress, the metrics reported in the CJ need to have the basic attributes of successful performance measures. As we previously reported, one of these attributes is clarity: a measure of performance has clarity when it is clearly stated and the name and definition are consistent with the methodology used for calculating it.[23] IRS officials told us the dates reported under "projected useful life of the current asset" are not based on a projection about the date at which the current assets will no longer be useful, but are instead arbitrary dates several years in the future and do not represent projections of the useful life of IT investments.[24] According to IRS officials, the years reported for most investments represent an arbitrary number of years, such as 3 or 5, after the current year. In some cases, the reported year may represent a projection of the useful life of the investment. However, according to an official in IRS's Information Technology office, different people are responsible for reporting on different investments, and they may report information according to different understandings of the meaning of the term "projected useful life of the current asset." The years reported in the CJ under "projected useful life of the current asset" for the 20 listed major IT investments are the following: 2017 (1 investment), 2018 (2 investments), 2019 (10 investments), 2020 (5 investments), 2021 (1 investment), and 2034 (1 investment).

As a result of this arbitrary process for reporting projected useful life, some of the information reported in the CJ is inconsistent with IRS's plans for its major IT investments. For example, according to IRS Information Technology officials, they plan to continue using the Return Review Program after the Electronic Fraud Detection System is no longer in use. However, the fiscal year 2016 CJ reports a "projected useful life of the current asset" of 2020 for the Return Review Program and a later date, 2021, for the Electronic Fraud Detection System. This sequence of dates is inconsistent with the plan to stop using the Electronic Fraud Detection System while continuing to use the Return Review Program. For another major IT investment, the Affordable Care Act Administration investment, IRS's Estimation Program Office has estimated costs for the investment through fiscal year 2026. This estimate indicates that IRS plans to use the Affordable Care Act Administration investment through fiscal year 2026. However, the CJ reports that the "projected useful life of the current asset" for the Affordable Care Act Administration investment is 2018.

Without clear and consistent definitions of these terms, the information IRS is reporting is of limited usefulness. As a result, Congress and other stakeholders do not have reliable information to make budget decisions about IT investments.

IRS IS TAKING STEPS TO IMPLEMENT GAO RECOMMENDATIONS, INCLUDING THOSE RELATED TO GREATER USE OF RETURN ON INVESTMENT DATA AND IMPROVEMENTS IN THE PPACA COST ESTIMATE

As of February 2015, we have 88 open recommendations and 8 matters for congressional consideration that could have financial implications if implemented. Since we last reviewed open recommendations to IRS and matters for congressional consideration during the fiscal year 2015 budget review, 19 recommendations to IRS were closed as implemented. For more information on open recommendations, see appendixes IV and V.

Additionally, we have conducted work related to 17 of the 35 legislative tax proposals included in the fiscal year 2016 CJ for IRS. For information about legislative proposals related to our open recommendations, see appendix VI.

Calculating and Using Return on Investment Data to Inform Resource Allocation Decisions Is a Long-Term Effort for IRS

In June 2014, we recommended that IRS use actual return on investment (ROI) calculations as part of resource allocation decisions.[25] IRS has made progress in response to this recommendation. Specifically, IRS's Research, Analysis, and Statistics Division has begun to estimate marginal direct revenue and marginal cost—the two key elements used to calculate return on investment data—attributable to specific compliance projects within its correspondence exam program. It plans to incorporate these estimates for use by SB/SE and Wage and Investment business unit managers for exam selection into the Exam Planning Scenario Tool, which is being developed by the Office of Compliance Analytics. That tool is intended ultimately to enable exam planners and business unit management to explore a wide range of potential exam plan scenarios and to compare the alternative effects on various enforcement objectives, including revenues collected and reduced taxpayer burden. Considerable work remains to be done on the multiple components of this long-term effort.

We also recommended that IRS calculate actual ROI for implemented initiatives.[26] IRS agreed that having this information would be useful. However, IRS noted that determining the impact of an initiative will always rely on estimates, as the results of an initiative are the difference between actual results and what would have occurred in the absence of the initiative, which cannot be measured. Given that IRS is unable to attribute revenues to specific employees hired under an initiative, officials believe that any feasible estimate would need to be based on numerous assumptions and, therefore would be too uncertain to be useful. For this reason, IRS does not consider this additional analysis an effective use of its scarce research resources. However, we believe that IRS should be able to provide some information to Congress, such as whether funds that were requested for initiatives were used in the manner that IRS originally proposed.

Updated PPACA Cost Estimate Showed Improvement and Met or Substantially Met Criteria in Three of Four Overall Categories, but Is Still Not Considered Reliable

IRS's PPACA cost estimate identifies the costs of planning, developing and implementing the IT systems needed to support its role in implementing PPACA. In February 2015, IRS released version 3 of the PPACA cost estimate as part of its ongoing practice to refine its cost estimate and address our prior recommendation. The cost estimate totals $2.72 billion (adjusted for inflation) from mid-fiscal year 2014 through fiscal year 2026; when prior years are included, the estimate increases to $3.43 billion from fiscal years 2010 through 2026 (adjusted for inflation). This updated cost estimate is a significant increase from the previous total of $1.89 billion (not adjusted for inflation) from fiscal years 2010 through 2026.[27] According to IRS officials, this increase is due to a change in the scope of PPACA implementation activities which resulted in additional releases. For example, the new releases respond to regulatory changes in the requirements for the Small Business Health Options Program, add in the cost of sending preliminary notices to employers not offering employee coverage, and take into account the implementation of the excise tax on high-cost health plans that will begin in 2018. However, IRS has not finalized the scope of work for Release 7.1 and beyond, which raises questions about IRS's ability to estimate costs for these releases.

According to the GAO *Cost Guide*, a reliable cost estimate must be comprehensive, well documented, accurate, and credible. [28] In September 2013, we reported that version 1 of IRS's cost estimate for PPACA did not fully meet best practices for a reliable cost estimate and recommended actions IRS should take to improve its cost estimate.[29] The updated cost estimate–version 3—reflects best practices to a greater extent, as shown in table 3. The cost estimate met or substantially met the criteria in three of four overall categories; however, a cost estimate must meet or substantially meet the criteria in all four overall categories to be considered reliable. From our assessment of version 1 of the cost estimate, of 20 sub-scores, 12 increased, 3 decreased, and 5 were constant. See appendix VII for a table of the sub-scores. Notably, IRS has improved documentation of how cost drivers for its sensitivity analysis were selected with the score improving from partially meets to meets. As outlined below, there are several areas related to our open recommendation where IRS could continue to improve the cost estimate to better meet best practices outlined in the GAO *Cost Guide*.

- **Earned value management:** We previously recommended that IRS use earned value management—a process for capturing actual costs and comparing them to estimated costs—to capture actual costs and use them as a basis for future updates. According to IRS officials, earned value management is not being used to track costs. Because of this, actual costs are not regularly being used to update the estimate and to determine where and why variances are occurring when there is still time to mitigate their effect on the program's cost and/or schedule in a manner that is consistent with best practices. This issue affects multiple elements of the accuracy of the cost estimate assessment.
- **Variance from prior estimate:** The estimate includes a general discussion of cost and schedule variance and gives an overview of how staffing and cost estimates have changed from the previous cost estimate; however, it does not offer a detailed discussion of the reasons why. A proper risk and uncertainty analysis is necessary to correctly assess the variability in the cost estimate due to program risks. In this area, the cost estimate improved from "minimally meets" to "partially meets."
- **Risk and uncertainty analysis:** IRS conducted a risk and uncertainty analysis but did not provide evidence that showed all of the steps they took to conduct the risk analysis, so we cannot verify that they followed best practices. Our assessment scored this element as

"partially meets"—which is the same as our assessment of the earlier version of the cost estimate.

- **Validating the estimate:** IRS did not obtain a second cost estimate and there is no program office estimate to use for comparison. The GAO Cost Guide specifies that producing two cost estimates that are independent of one another is a best practice because the second cost estimate can validate the first and provide an unbiased test of whether the original cost estimate is reasonable. Our assessment scored this element as "minimally meets"—which is the same as our assessment of the earlier version of the cost estimate.

Table 3. Overall Assessment of Patient Protection and Affordable Care Act Cost Estimate Alignment with Best Practices

		Overall Assessment		
Best Practice	**Description**	**October 2010[a]**	**Version 1 December 2012**	**Version 3 February 2015**
Comprehensive	A comprehensive cost estimate ensures that cost elements are neither omitted nor double counted, and all cost-influencing ground rules and assumptions are detailed.	◑	◕	◕
Well documented	A well-documented cost estimate thoroughly documents the process, including source data, clearly detailed calculations and results, and explanations of why particular references were chosen.	◑	◕	●

		Overall Assessment		
Best Practice	**Description**	**October 2010[a]**	**Version 1 December 2012**	**Version 3 February 2015**
Accurate	An accurate cost estimate is unbiased and is not overly conservative or optimistic. It is based on an assessment of most likely costs.	◑	◑	◕
Credible	A credible cost estimate discusses any limitations of the analysis because of uncertainty or bias surrounding data or assumptions used in the cost estimating process.	◔	◑	◑

Key: ● = Meets—IRS provided complete evidence that satisfies the entire criterion; ◕= Substantially meets—IRS provided evidence that satisfies a large portion of the criterion; ◑= Partially meets—IRS provided evidence that satisfies about half of the criterion; ◔= Minimally meets—IRS provided evidence that satisfies a small portion of the criterion; ○ = Does not meet—IRS provided no evidence that satisfies any of the criterion.

Source: GAO analysis of IRS February 2015 PPACA cost estimate (version 3). | GAO-15-624

[a]IRS completed a cost estimate in October 2010 that it did not label with a version number.

CONCLUSION

Over the last 5 years, IRS took steps to manage budget reductions; however, many were short-term actions, such as strictly limiting hiring and curtailing overtime. Some of these actions could result in future disruptions in taxpayer services and diminished administration of our tax system. IRS has some flexibility in how it allocates resources—including user fee revenue—within and across business units to achieve its mission and goals. IRS reprioritized many activities since fiscal year 2010 to address budget reductions. Activities and services that were scaled back remain important and may have benefits, including a positive return on investment or enhanced compliance with the tax system. IRS tradeoffs could lead to negative outcomes such as reduced program effectiveness and increased risk to IRS and the federal government. This highlights the importance of Congress and IRS working together to reexamine IRS's mission and priorities. To improve transparency and inform decision-making, accurate information on IT investments in the CJ is imperative.

RECOMMENDATIONS FOR EXECUTIVE ACTION

To enhance the budget process and to improve transparency, we recommend the Commissioner of Internal Revenue take the following actions:

- Implement internal controls to ensure the accuracy of information on major information technology investments reported in the annual congressional justification, such as obligations data.
- To the extent possible, report information about major information technology investments in the congressional justification in accordance with the standard terms published by the Comptroller General in the Budget Glossary (GAO-05-734SP).
- When using key terms that are not defined in the Budget Glossary or in OMB guidance, or when using a modification of these terms, provide definitions of key terms used to report information about major information technology investments in the congressional justification.

AGENCY COMMENTS AND OUR EVALUATION

We provided a draft of this report to the Commissioner of Internal Revenue for comment. In written comments reproduced in appendix VIII, IRS agreed with our recommendations. IRS plans to conduct a comprehensive review of its capital planning and investment control activities, with particular emphasis on investment controls. As part of this review, IRS plans to identify any gaps in the use of standard terms, make recommendations for changes to standard terms, and define terms not included in the Budget Glossary. We agree that identifying gaps and implementing changes to enhance the budget will improve data quality. IRS also provided technical comments on our draft report, which we incorporated as appropriate.

James R. McTigue, Jr.
Director, Tax Issues Strategic Issues

APPENDIX I: IRS FUNDING AND FTE DATA FROM FISCAL YEAR 2009 THROUGH FISCAL YEAR 2016

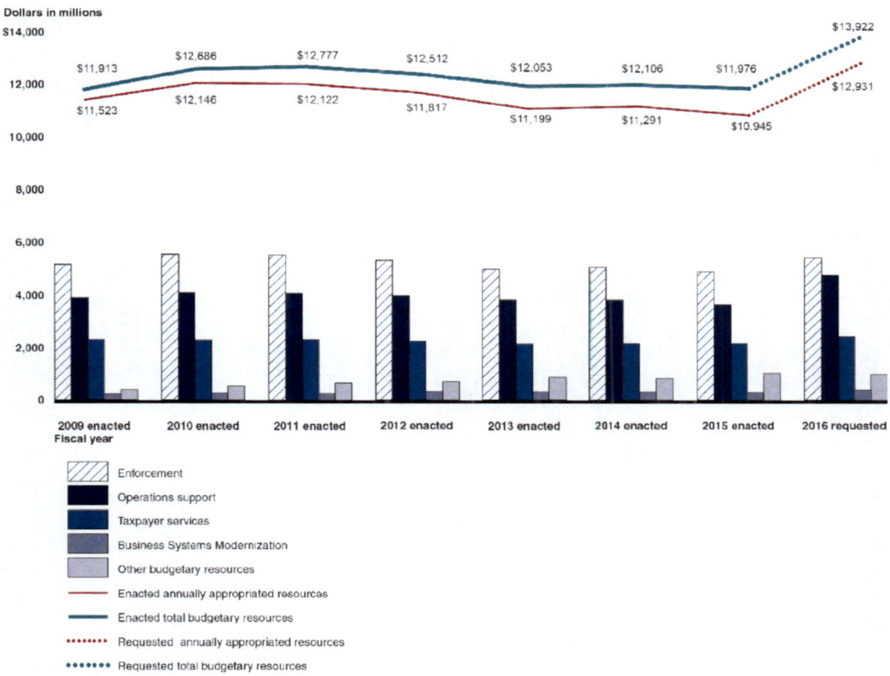

Source: Congressional justification for IRS, fiscal years 2011 through 2016. | GAO-15-624

Note: All numbers in the figure are nominal and not adjusted for inflation. IRS funded government-wide wage and salary and employer health-insurance premium increases for its employees over this period.

Figure 2. Fiscal Years 2009 through 2015 Enacted and Fiscal Year 2016 Budget Request for IRS (Dollars in Millions).

Table 4. Fiscal Years 2009 through 2015 Enacted and Fiscal Year 2016 Budget Request for IRS

Dollars in millions										
Appropriations account	**Fiscal year 2009 enacted**	**Fiscal year 2010 enacted**	**Fiscal year 2011 enacted**	**Fiscal year 2012 enacted**	**Fiscal year 2013 enacted[a]**	**Fiscal year 2014 enacted**	**Fiscal year 2015 enacted**	**Fiscal year 2016 requested**	**Dollar change fiscal year 2015 enacted compared to fiscal year 2016 requested**	**Percent change fiscal year 2015 enacted compared to fiscal year 2016 requested**
Enforcement	$5,117	$5,504	$5,493	$5,299	$4,949	$5,022	$4,860	$5,400	$540	11.11
Operations support	3,867	4,084	4,057	3,947	3,801	3,799	3,638	4,743	1,105	30.36
Taxpayer services	2,293	2,279	2,293	2,240	2,136	2,157	2,157	2,409	252	11.70
Business Systems Modernization	230	264	263	330	313	313	290	379	89	30.75
Health Insurance Tax Credit Administration (HITCA)[b]	15	16	15	0	0	0	0	0	0	0
Subtotal	11,523	12,146	12,122	11,817	11,199	11,291	10,945	12,931	1,986	18.15
Other resources, such as user fees	390	539	655	695	855	815	1,031	991	-40	-3.86
Total funding available for obligations	$11,913	$12,686	$12,777	$12,512	$12,053	$12,106	$11,976	$13,922	$1,946	16.25

Source: Congressional justifications for IRS, fiscal years 2011 through 2016. | GAO-15-624

Notes: Dollars are nominal and not adjusted for inflation, and numbers may not add due to rounding.

[a]Fiscal year 2013 enacted represents the operating level after applying across-the-board rescission and reductions required by sequestration.

[b]In fiscal year 2012 and thereafter, amounts appropriated for HITCA, which had been a separate account, were moved to the Taxpayer Services appropriation.

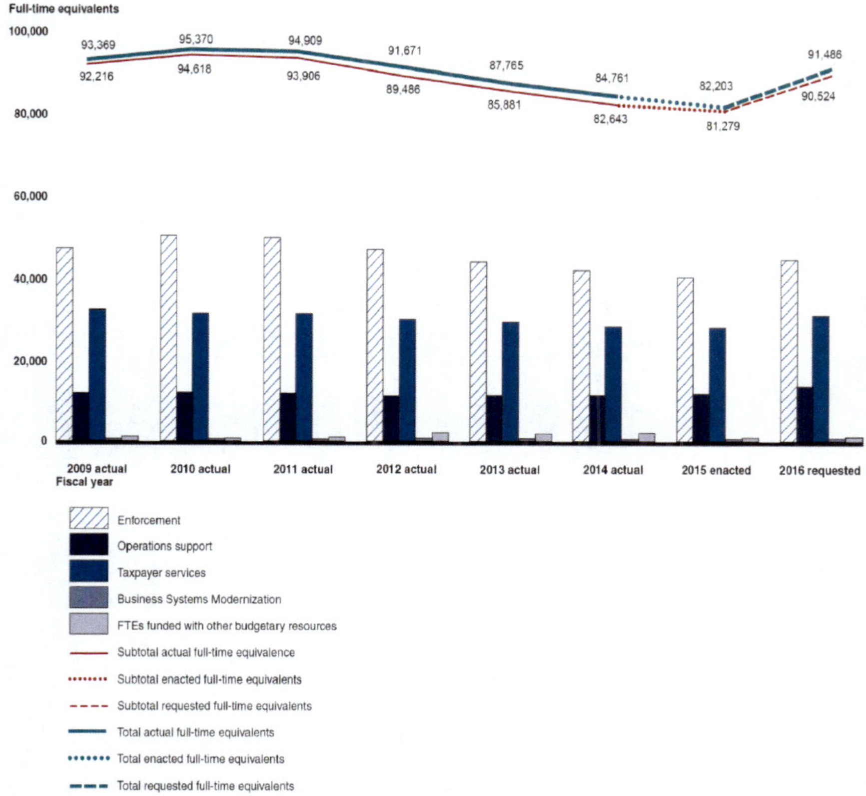

Source: Congressional justifications for IRS, fiscal years 2011 through 2016. | GAO-15-624

Figure 3. IRS Full-time Equivalents, Fiscal Years 2009 through 2014 Actual, 2015 Enacted, and 2016 Requested.

Table 5. IRS Full-time Equivalents, Fiscal Years 2009 through 2014 Actual, 2015 Enacted, and 2016 Requested

Appropriations account	Fiscal year 2009 actual	Fiscal year 2010 actual	Fiscal year 2011 actual	Fiscal year 2012 actual	Fiscal year 2013 actual	Fiscal year 2014 actual	Fiscal year 2015 enacted	Fiscal year 2016 requested	FTE change fiscal year 2015 enacted compared to fiscal year 2016 requested	Percent change fiscal year 2015 enacted compared to fiscal year 2016 requested
Enforcement	47,361	50,400	49,920	47,189	44,174	42,119	40,564	44,800	4,236	10.4
Operations support	12,101	12,262	12,103	11,499	11,610	11,652	12,043	13,863	1,820	15.1
Taxpayer services	32,422	31,607	31,574	30,236	29,646	28,535	28,274	31,285	3,011	10.7
Business Systems Modernization	322	337	309	562	451	337	398	576	178	44.7
Health Insurance Tax Credit Administration (HITCA)[a]	10	12	0	0	0	0	0	0	0	0
Subtotal	92,216	94,618	93,906	89,486	85,881	82,643	81,279	90,524	9,245	11.4
Other resources, such as user fees	1,153	752	1,003	2,185	1,884	2,118	924	962	38	4.1
Total	93,369	95,370	94,909	91,671	87,765	84,761	82,203	91,486	9,283	11.3

Source: Congressional justifications for IRS, fiscal years 2011 through 2016. | GAO-15-624

[a]The administrative resources for HITCA were moved to the Taxpayer Services appropriation.

APPENDIX II: FIGURE 1 - FISCAL YEAR 2014 OBLIGATIONS BY FUND CENTER AND PERCENTAGE CHANGE FROM FISCAL YEAR 2010

Fund center	Taxpayer services	Enforcement	Operations support	Business Systems Modernization	Total fiscal year 2014 obligations	Total fiscal year 2010 obligations	Percentchange inobligations,fiscal year 2010 to2 014
Large Business and International	$7	$845	$8	$0	$860	$941	-9
Small Business/Self Employed	22	2,219	10	0	2,250	2,613	-14
Wage and Investment	1,795	432	49	0	2,276	2,411	-6
Wage and Investment - Stewardship	69	0	208	0	276	373	-26
Tax Exempt and Government Entities	11	243	1	0	256	277	-8
Appeals	0	216	0	0	216	247	-12
Counsel	12	320	0	0	332	369	-10
Criminal Investigation	0	586	0	0	586	619	-5
Taxpayer Advocate Service	212	0	0	0	212	222	-4
Communications and Liaison	0	0	20	0	20	26	-22
Agency-Wide Shared Services (AWSS)	0	0	243	0	243	290	-16
AWSS - Stewardship	0	0	964	0	964	1,081	-11
Information Technology	0	0	1,744	145	1,890	1,980	-5
Executive Leadership and Direction	17	54	111	0	182	109	67
Privacy, Governmental Liaison and Disclosurea	0	0	51	0	51	- a	- a
Human Capital Office	0	0	137	0	137	182	-25
Human Capital Office - Corporate Programs	0	0	28	0	28	60	-53
Chief Financial Officer	0	0	58	0	58	58	1

Source: GAO analysis of IRS obligations data. | GAO-15-624

Note: Numbers may not add due to rounding.

[a]Privacy, Governmental Liaison and Disclosure was not established in fiscal year 2010 therefore obligations data did not exist and a percent change was not calculated.

This table does not include obligations less than $1 million. In fiscal year 2014, 4 fund centers obligated less than $1 million from additional accounts: Counsel ($222,000 from Operations Support); Communications & Liaison ($92,000 from Taxpayer Services and $6,000 from Enforcement); Criminal Investigations ($38,000 from Operations Support); and Privacy, Governmental Liaison and Disclosure ($29,000 from Enforcement).

APPENDIX III: SUMMARY OF MAJOR INFORMATION TECHNOLOGY INVESTMENTS REPORTED IN IRS'S FISCAL YEAR 2016 CONGRESSIONAL JUSTIFICATION

Dollars in Millions				
Investment name	**Description**	**Start date of investment**	**Obligations from start date through end of fiscal year 2014**	**Plannedspending forfiscal year2015**
Account Management Services	Enhances customer support by providing applications that enable IRS employees to access, validate, and update individual taxpayer accounts on demand.	2009	$120.4	$17.7
Affordable Care Act Administration	Encompasses the planning, development, and implementation of IT systems needed to support IRS's tax administration responsibilities associated with the Patient Protection and Affordable Care Act.	2010	$992.4	$373.0

Dollars in Millions				
Investment name	**Description**	**Start date of investment**	**Obligations from start date through end of fiscal year 2014**	**Plannedspending forfiscal year2015**
Customer Account Data Engine 2	Provides timely access to authoritative individual taxpayer account information and enhances IRS's ability to address security, financial material weaknesses, and long-term architectural planning and viability.	2009	$789.3	$130.9
Electronic Fraud Detection System	Detects fraud at the time that tax returns are filed in order to eliminate the issuance of fraudulent tax refunds.	1996	$128.3	$18.6
e-Services	Comprises several web-based self-assisted services that are intended to allow authorized individuals to do business with the IRS electronically.	1999	$183.1	$5.3
Foreign Account Tax Compliance Act	Intended to implement provisions of the Foreign Account Tax Compliance Act regarding financial institutions reporting to IRS information about financial accounts held by U.S. taxpayers, or foreign entities in which U.S. taxpayers hold a substantial ownership interest.	2011	$58.1	$62.6
Individual Master File	Represents the authoritative data source for individual tax account data, supporting other IRS information systems and providing a critical component of IRS's ability to process tax returns.	1999	$128.6	$12.9

(Continued)

Dollars in Millions				
Investment name	**Description**	**Start date of investment**	**Obligations from start date through end of fiscal year 2014**	**Plannedspending forfiscal year2015**
Information Reporting and Document Matching	Intended to establish a new business information matching program in order to increase voluntary compliance and accurate income reporting.	2009	$99.5	$5.5
Integrated Customer Communication Environment	Includes several projects that are intended to simplify voluntary compliance using telephone applications, Internet, and other computer technology.	1992	$496.3	$13.1
Integrated Data Retrieval System	Intended to provide systemic review, improve consistency in case control, alleviate staffing needs, issue notices to taxpayers, and allow taxpayers to see status of refunds.	1973	$217.1	$16.0
Integrated Financial System	Provides budget, payroll, accounts payable/receivable, general ledger functions, and financial reporting; also used to manage budgets by fiscal year.		2001	$429.3
Integrated Submission and Remittance Processing System	Processes paper tax returns, and updates tax forms to comply with tax law changes.		1998	$153.6
IRS End User Systems and Services	Supports products and services necessary for daily functions for IRS employees at headquarters and field sites.		1970	$883.1

Dollars in Millions				
Investment name	**Description**	**Start date of investment**	**Obligations from start date through end of fiscal year 2014**	**Plannedspending forfiscal year2015**
IRS Main Frames and Servers Services and Support	Supports the design, development, and deployment of server storage infrastructures, software, databases, and operating systems.		1970	$4,649.3
IRS Telecommunications Systems and Support	Supports IRS's broad and local network infrastructure such as servers, and switches for voice, data, and video servicing of IRS sites.		1970	$1,279.1
IRS.gov - Portal Environment	Provides web-based services to internal and external users, such as IRS employees and other government agencies, taxpayers, and business partners.		1996	$559.1
Modernized e-File	Provides a secure web-based platform for electronic tax filing of individual and business tax and information returns by registered Electronic Return Originators.		2001	$424.9
Return Review Program	Aims to maximize detection of fraud, including identity theft fraud, at the time that tax returns are filed, to eliminate issuance of questionable refunds.		2010	$151.0
Service Center Recognition/Image Processing System	Used as a data capture, management, and image storage system using high-speed scanning and digital imaging to convert data from the 940, 941, K-1, and paper returns from Information Returns Processing into an electronic format.		1991	$167.7

(Continued)

Dollars in Millions				
Investment name	**Description**	**Start date of investment**	**Obligations from start date through end of fiscal year 2014**	**Plannedspending forfiscal year2015**
Web Applications	Provides online tools for taxpayers, such as Where's My Refund and Get Transcript; supports search function and design of IRS.gov.		2013	$2.2

Source: IRS's fiscal year 2016 congressional justification and IRS budget obligations data. | GAO-15-624

Note: In prior years we reported the life-cycle costs and projected useful life of each major IT investment; however, we are not reporting those data because we found them to be unclear. According to Department of the Treasury guidance, a major investment is one that costs $10 million in either the current year or budget year, or $50 million over the 5-year period extending from the prior year through 2 years after the budget year. OMB has instructed agencies not to categorize IT capital planning and Chief Information Officer function investments as major IT investments. We determined that the data reported in this table were sufficiently reliable based upon written explanations and documentation submitted to us by officials from IRS and the Department of the Treasury responsible for maintaining the systems from which these data were obtained.

APPENDIX IV: GAO BUDGET-RELATED RECOMMENDATIONS TO IRS THAT REMAIN OPEN

Report	Recommendations	Benefit	Status
GAO-12-603	*Conduct cost-effectiveness analyses* Ensure cost-effectiveness analyses are conducted for future significant investments when there are alternative approaches for achieving a given benefit, such as for any new significant Patient Protection and Affordable Care Act (PPACA) projects.	Without cost-effectiveness analyses, budget decision makers do not have information to compare alternatives and it may be difficult to determine the best use of resources.	As of February 2015, IRS officials reported that for the fiscal year 2017 budget formulation process, they have developed new instructions and procedures for conducting cost-effectiveness analyses, which include considering trade-offs and alternatives of proposed investments. Also, they plan to conduct cost-effectiveness analyses for future significant nonenforcement initiatives when there are alternative approaches to achieving a given benefit and there is sufficient time to conduct the analyses, according to officials. IRS actions are consistent with what we recommended in June 2012; however, we cannot obtain documentation for the fiscal year 2017 budget formulation process because it is considered pre-decisional. When the data is available we will assess it.

(Continued)

Report	***Recommendations***	**Benefit**	**Status**
GAO-12-603	*Develop a quantitative measure of scope* At a minimum, develop a quantitative measure of scope for its major IT investments, in order to have complete information on the performance of these investments.	A quantitative measure of scope is a good practice as it provides an objective measure of whether an investment delivered the functionality that was paid for.	No executive action taken. IRS officials stated that they agreed with the recommendation when we made it in June 2012. However, in October 2013, IRS said it did not plan to develop a quantitative measure of scope for its major information technology investments. In June 2014 and again in March 2015, IRS reported that it has practices and processes in place that provide performance information on its investments, including quarterly reports to Congress and a baseline change requestprocess. However, neither approach includes a quantitative measure. For this reason, we maintain that the recommendation is still warranted.

Report	*Recommendations*	Benefit	Status
GAO-13-835	*Improve budget formulation guidance* Improve guidance given to business units for the pre-selection budget formulation process, emphasizing the importance of information on the estimated impact—qualitative or quantitative—of proposed budget initiatives.	Expanding internal guidance for pre-selection budget formulation templates facilitates more complete information for internal budget decision-making.	IRS updated budget formulation guidance for the fiscal year 2016 budget formulation process. Guidance instructed business units to identify the expected benefit of the proposed budget initiative. We requested examples of completed templates to confirm the guidance was implemented by business units; however, as of mid-May, 2015 we have not received them. Once we receive the data, we will assess it.
GAO-13-835	*Further refine updates to the PPACA cost estimate* Improve the accuracy and credibility of future updates to the PPACA cost estimate by taking the following actions to more closely follow best practices outlined in the GAO Cost Guide: •Use earned value management to capture actual costs and use them as a basis for future updates. •Explain why variances occurred between the current estimate and previous estimates.	Developing a cost estimate that meets additional best practices, will foster accountability, improve insight, and provide objective information.	In February 2015, IRS released version 3 of the PPACA cost estimate, which reflects best practices to a greater extent, as shown in appendix VII; however, IRS has taken action on only 2 of 5 elements of the recommendation. IRS has improved documentation of how cost drivers for its sensitivity analysis were selected with the score improving from "partially meets" to "meets." While the score for variance from prior estimate improved, it went from "minimally meets" to "partially meets."

(Continued)

Report	*Recommendations*	Benefit	Status
	•Conduct future risk and uncertainty analyses consistent with best practices, and develop and document plans to address risks. •Validate the original cost estimate by preparing a second, independent cost estimate.		IRS has not improved its practicesrelated to the use of earned value management, risk and uncertainty analysis, or validating the estimate.
GAO-14-605	*Develop a long-term strategy* Develop a long-term strategy to address operations amidst an uncertain budget environment. As part of the strategy, IRS should take steps to improve its efficiency, including •Reexamine programs, related processes, and organizational structures to determine whether they are effectively and efficiently achieving the IRS mission. •Streamline or consolidate management or operational processes and functions to make them more cost-effective.	Developing a long-term strategy will enhance budget planning and improve decision making and accountability.	In June 2014, IRS established the Planning, Programming, and Audit Coordination office to, in part, improve long-term planning for resource allocation and decision making, and strategic planning. The Planning, Programming, and Audit Coordination office efforts will inform the fiscal year 2017 budget formulation process. We will continue to monitor IRS's progress and will assess a strategy once it is developed.

Report	***Recommendations***	Benefit	Status
GAO-14-605	*Enhance calculation and use of actual return on investment (ROI) data* •Calculate actual ROI for implemented initiatives, compare the actual ROI to projected ROI, and provide the comparison to budget decision makers for initiatives where IRS allocated resources. •Use actual ROI calculations as part of resource allocation decisions.	Enhanced calculation of ROI provides greater insight on the productivity of a program and can inform decision making.	IRS's Research, Analysis, and Statistics Division has begun to estimate marginal direct revenues and marginal costs attributable to specific compliance projects within its correspondence exam program. It plans to use these estimates to inform potential exams, but considerable work remains in this long-term effort. Additionally, while IRS agreed that having actual ROI data would be useful, it did not believe it could determine a feasible estimate. We believe that IRS should be able to provide some information such as whether funds requested were used in the manner originallyproposed. We will continue to monitor IRS's progress.

Source: GAO analysis of IRS data. | GAO-15-624

Appendix V: List of Open Matters for Congressional Consideration and Recommendations to IRS That Could Result in Potential Savings or Increased Revenues

The 44 GAO products listed below contain 88 recommendations and 8 matters for congressional consideration that could have a financial impact if implemented.

Table 6. List of Open Matters for Congressional Consideration and Recommendations to IRS

Report Title and Number	Potential Financial Impact
Enhancing budget requests and implementing Patient Protection and Affordable Care Act (PPACA)	
IRS 2014 Budget: Improvements Made to Budget Request and Cost Estimate, but Further Actions Needed (GAO-13-835)	Increase Savings, Indirect Financial Benefit
IRS 2013 Budget: Continuing to Improve Information on Program Costs and Results Could Aid in Resource Decision Making (GAO-12-603)	Increase Savings, Indirect Financial Benefit
Enhancing electronic filing	
E-Filing Tax Returns: Penalty Authority and Digitizing More Paper Return Data Could Increase Benefits (GAO-12-33)	Increase Savings, Increase Savings and Revenue
Electronic Tax Return Filing: Improvements Can Be Made before Mandate Becomes Fully Implemented (GAO-11-344)	Increase Savings
Enhancing electronic filing and improving accuracy of paid preparers	
Tax Administration: Many Taxpayers Rely on Tax Software and IRS Needs to Assess Associated Risks (GAO-09-297)	Increase Financial Benefit
Enhancing internal controls	
Management Report: Improvements Are Needed to Enhance the Internal Revenue Service's Internal Controls (GAO-14-433R)	Indirect Financial Benefit

Report Title and Number	Potential Financial Impact
Management Report: Improvements Are Needed to Enhance the Internal Revenue Service's Internal Controls (GAO-13-420R)	Increase Savings, Indirect Financial Benefit
Enhancing online taxpayer services	
IRS Website: Long-Term Strategy Needed to Improve Interactive Services (GAO-13-435)	Increase Savings, Indirect Financial Benefit
Enhancing private pension disclosures	
Private Pensions: Targeted Revisions Could Improve Usefulness of Form 5500 Information (GAO-14-441)	Increase Savings
Private Pensions: Clarity of Required Reports and Disclosures Could Be Improved (GAO-14-92)	Increase Financial Benefit
Enhancing oversight of charitable organizations	
Tax-Exempt Organizations: Better Compliance Indicators and Data, and More Collaboration with State Regulators Would Strengthen Oversight of Charitable Organizations (GAO-15-164)	Increase Savings
Enhancing taxpayer services	
2012 Tax Filing: IRS Faces Challenges Providing Service to Taxpayers and Could Collect Balances Due More Effectively (GAO-13-156)	Increase Savings and Revenue
2011 Tax Filing: Processing Gains, but Taxpayer Assistance Could Be Enhanced by More Self-Service Tools (GAO-12-176)	Increase Savings and Revenue
Enhancing treatment of appraisals issues	
Appraised Values on Tax Returns: Burdens on Taxpayers Could Be Reduced and Selected Practices Improved (GAO-12-608)	Increase Savings, Increase Savings and Revenue
Enhancing verification of tax returns	
Tax Refunds: IRS Is Exploring Verification Improvements, but Needs to Better Manage Risks (GAO-13-515)	Indirect Financial Benefit
Expanding use of math error authority or third party data	
2011 Tax Filing: IRS Dealt with Challenges to Date but Needs Additional Authority to Verify Compliance (GAO-11-481)	Increase Revenue

(Continued)

Report Title and Number	Potential Financial Impact
Recovery Act: IRS Quickly Implemented Tax Provisions, but Reporting and Enforcement Improvements Are Needed (GAO-10-349)	Increase Savings and Revenue
2009 Tax Filing Season: IRS Met Many 2009 Goals, but Telephone Access Remained Low, and Taxpayer Service and Enforcement Could Be Improved (GAO-10-225)	Increase Revenue, Increase Savings and Revenue
Tax Administration: IRS's 2008 Filing Season Generally Successful Despite Challenges, although IRS Could Expand Enforcement during Returns Processing (GAO-09-146)	Increase Savings and Revenue
Implementing Information Reporting and Document Matching (IRDM) system	
IRS Management: Cost Estimate for New Information Reporting System Needs to be Made More Reliable (GAO-12-59)	Indirect Financial Benefit
Information Reporting: IRS Could Improve Cost Basis and Transaction Settlement Reporting Implementation (GAO-11-557)	Indirect Financial Benefit
Implementing Patient Protection and Affordable Care Act (PPACA)	
Patient Protection and Affordable Care Act: IRS Should Expand Its Strategic Approach to Implementation (GAO-11-719)	Indirect Financial Benefit
Improving accuracy of returns completed by paid preparers	
Paid Tax Return Preparers: In a Limited Study, Preparers Made Significant Errors (GAO-14-467T)	Indirect Financial Benefit
Improving allocation of enforcement resources	
IRS 2015 Budget: Long-Term Strategy and Return on Investment Data Needed to Better Manage Budget Uncertainty and Set Priorities (GAO-14-605)	Increase Savings and Revenue
Tax Gap: IRS Could Significantly Increase Revenues by Better Targeting Enforcement Resources (GAO-13-151)	Increase Revenue

Report Title and Number	Potential Financial Impact
Improving administration of installment agreements	
2013 Tax Filing Season: IRS Needs to Do More to Address the Growing Imbalance between the Demand for Services and Resources (GAO-14-133)	Increase Savings
Improving collection of unpaid taxes from Medicaid providers	
Medicaid: Providers in Three States with Unpaid Federal Taxes Received Over $6 Billion in Medicaid Reimbursements (GAO-12-857)	Increase Savings
Improving corporate tax compliance	
Corporate Tax Compliance: IRS Should Determine Whether Its Streamlined Corporate Audit Process Is Meeting Its Goals (GAO-13-662)	Increase Savings
Improving examinations of tax returns	
Tax Administration: IRS Could Improve Examinations by Adopting Certain Research Program Practices (GAO-13-480)	Increase Revenue
Improving individual or corporate tax compliance	
Partnerships and S Corporations: IRS Needs to Improve Information to Address Tax Noncompliance (GAO-14-453)	Increase Revenue, Increase Savings and Revenue
Virtual Economies and Currencies: Additional IRS Guidance Could Reduce Tax Compliance Risks (GAO-13-516)	Increase Revenue
Federal Tax Collection: Potential for Using Passport Issuance to Increase Collection of Unpaid Taxes (GAO-11-272)	Increase Revenue
Improving management of enforcement audits	
Large Partnerships: With Growing Number of Partnerships, IRS Needs to Improve Audit Efficiency (GAO-14-732)	Increase Revenue, Increase Savings and Revenue,Indirect Financial Benefit
IRS Correspondence Audits: Better Management Could Improve Tax Compliance and Reduce Taxpayer Burden (GAO-14-479)	Increase Savings, Indirect Financial Benefit

(Continued)

Report Title and Number	Potential Financial Impact
Improving management of information technology (IT) investments	
Investment Management: IRS Has a Strong Oversight Process but Needs to Improve How It Continues Funding Ongoing Investments (GAO-11-587)	Increase Savings, Indirect Financial Benefit
Improving offshore compliance	
Offshore Tax Evasion: IRS Has Collected Billions of Dollars, But May be Missing Continued Evasion (GAO-13-318)	Increase Revenue
Improving rental real estate compliance	
Tax Gap: Actions That Could Improve Rental Real Estate Reporting Compliance (GAO-08-956)	Increase Revenue
Improving sole proprietors' compliance	
Tax Gap: Limiting Sole Proprietor Loss Deductions Could Improve Compliance but Would Also Limit Some Legitimate Losses (GAO-09-815)	Indirect Financial Benefit
Improving tax credit administration	
Small Employer Health Tax Credit: Factors Contributing to Low Use and Complexity (GAO-12-549)	Increase Savings and Revenue
Improving third party compliance	
Tax Gap: IRS Could Do More to Promote Compliance by Third Parties with Miscellaneous Income Reporting Requirements (GAO-09-238)	Increase Revenue, Indirect Financial Benefit
Preventing tax refund fraud	
Identify and Tax Fraud: Enhanced Authentication Could Combat Refund Fraud, but IRS Lacks an Estimate of Costs, Benefits and Risks (GAO-15-119)	Increase Savings and Revenue
Identity Theft: Additional Actions Could Help IRS Combat The Large, Evolving Threat Of Refund Fraud (GAO-14-633)	Increase Savings, Increase Savings and Revenue

Report Title and Number	Potential Financial Impact
Promoting effective use of third-party data	
Tax Gap: IRS Has Modernized Its Business Nonfiler Program but Could Benefit from More Evaluation and Use of Third-Party Data (GAO-10-950)	Increase Revenue
Promoting retirement savings while reducing noncompliance	
Individual Retirement Accounts: IRS Could Bolster Enforcement on Multimillion Dollar Accounts, but More Direction from Congress Is Needed (GAO-15-16)	Increase Revenue, Increase Savings and Revenue,Indirect Financial Benefit
Reducing tax evasion	
Tax Gap: IRS Can Improve Efforts to Address Tax Evasion by Networks of Businesses and Related Entities (GAO-10-968)	Indirect Financial Benefit

Source: GAO analysis. | GAO-15-624

APPENDIX VI: IRS LEGISLATIVE TAX PROPOSALS RELATED TO PRIOR GAO WORK

We conducted work related to 17 of the 35 legislative tax proposals included in the fiscal year 2016 congressional justification for IRS.

Table 7. IRS Legislative Tax Proposals Related to Prior GAO Work

Dollars in Millions			
IRS legislative proposal related to prior GAO work	**Projected costs over 3 years**	**Projected revenues over 10 years**	**Related GAO reports**
Modify reporting of tuition expenses and scholarships on Form 1098-T, Tuition Statement	$0.2	-$172	GAO-10-225
Provide for reciprocal reporting of information in connection with the implementation of the Foreign Account Tax Compliance Act.	4.2	No revenue effect	GAO-12-484; GAO-12-403

Table 7. (Continued)

Dollars in Millions			
IRS legislative proposal related to prior GAO work	**Projected costs over 3 years**	**Projected revenues over 10 years**	**Related GAO reports**
Require greater electronic filing of returns	0.6	10a	GAO-14-453
Increase certainty with respect to worker classification	1.9	10,170	GAO-09-717
Increase levy authority for payments to Medicare providers with delinquent tax debt	0.1	514	GAO-12-857
Streamline audit and adjustment procedures for large partnerships	2.5	2,407	GAO-14-732; GAO-14-746T
Require taxpayers who prepare their returns electronically but file their returns on paper to print their returns with a scannable code	14.6	10a	GAO-08-38; GAO-09-297
Allow IRS to absorb credit and debit card processing fees for certain tax payments	9.6	20	GAO-10-11
Provide IRS with greater flexibility to address correctable errors	1.4	639	GAO-09-146; GAO-09-1026; GAO-10-225; GAO-11-481
Authorize the Department of Treasury to require additional information to be included in electronically filed Form 5500 annual reports and electronic filing of certain other employee benefit plan reports	11.2	10a	GAO-05-491
Impose a penalty on failure to comply with electronic filing requirements	2.5	10a	GAO-12-33

Dollars in Millions			
IRS legislative proposal related to prior GAO work	**Projected costs over 3 years**	**Projected revenues over 10 years**	**Related GAO reports**
Improve the whistleblower program	0.0	Negligible revenue effect	GAO-11-683
Index all penalties for inflation	.8	Negligible revenue effect	GAO-07-1062
Extend paid preparer Earned Income Tax Credit (EITC) due diligence requirements to the child tax credit	20.2	Negligible revenue effect	GAO-02-290R; GAO-05-92; GAO-07-1110
Combat tax-related identity theft	2.7	Negligible revenue effect	GAO-14-633; GAO-13-132T; GAO-15-119
Explicitly provide that the Department of Treasury and IRS have authority to regulate all paid return preparers	Not available	427	GAO-14-467T;GAO-06-563T;GAO-11-336; GAO-08-781
Rationalize tax return filing due dates so they are staggered	1.0	1,630	GAO-13-515

Source: GAO analysis based on IRS fiscal year 2016 congressional justification and Department of the Treasury, General Explanations of the Administrations Fiscal Year 2016 Revenue Proposals (Washington, D.C.: February 2015). | GAO-15-624

[a]The Department of Treasury includes this legislative proposal under "Enhance Electronic Filing of Returns" and provides a single projected revenue for this proposal, as well as several others.

APPENDIX VII: PPACA COST ESTIMATE ASSESSMENT

The updated PPACA cost estimate–version 3—reflects best practices to a greater extent, as shown below. The cost estimate met or substantially met the criteria in three of four overall categories; however, a cost estimate must meet or substantially meet the criteria in all four overall categories to be considered reliable. Of 20 subscores, 12 increased, 3 decreased, and 5 were constant from our assessment of version 1 of the cost estimate.

Table 8. Sub Scores of PPACA Cost Estimate Alignment with Best Practices

	Sub-scores	
Characteristic and Best Practice	**Version 1 December 2012**	**Version 3 February 2015**
Comprehensive		
The cost estimate includes all life cycle costs.	●	◑
The cost estimate completely defines the program, reflects the current schedule, and is technically reasonable.	◕	●
The cost estimate work breakdown structure is product-oriented, traceable to the statement of work/objective, and at an appropriate level of detail to ensure that cost elements are neither omitted nor double-counted.	●	◕
The estimate documents all cost-influencing ground rules and assumptions.	◕	●
Well documented		
The documentation should capture the source data used, the reliability of the data, and how the data were normalized.	◕	●
The documentation describes in sufficient detail the calculations performed and the estimating methodology used to derive each element's cost.	◕	●
The documentation describes step by step how the estimate was developed so that a cost analyst unfamiliar with the program could understand what was done and replicate it.	◕	●
The documentation discusses the technical baseline description and the data in the baseline is consistent with the estimate.	●	●
The documentation provides evidence that the cost estimate was reviewed and accepted by management.	◕	◕
Accurate		
The cost estimate results are unbiased, not overly conservative or optimistic, and are based on an assessment of most likely costs.	◕	●
The estimate has been adjusted properly for inflation.	◑	●

Characteristic and Best Practice	Sub-scores	
	Version 1 December 2012	**Version 3 February 2015**
The estimate contains few, if any, minor mistakes.	◕	◕
The cost estimate is regularly updated to reflect significant changes in the program so that it is always reflecting current status.	◑	◕
Variances between planned and actual costs are documented, explained, and reviewed.	◔	◑
The estimate is based on a historical record of cost estimating and actual experiences from other comparable programs.	◕	●
The estimating technique for each cost element was used appropriately.	◕	●
Credible		
The cost estimate includes a sensitivity analysis that identifies a range of possible costs based on varying major assumptions, parameters, and data inputs.	◑	●
A risk and uncertainty analysis was conducted that quantified the imperfectly understood risks and identified the effects of changing key cost driver assumptions and factors.	◑	◑
Major cost elements were cross checked to see whether results were similar.	◕	◑
An independent cost estimate was conducted by a group outside the acquiring organization to determine whether other estimating methods produce similar results.	◔	◔

Key: ● = Meets—IRS provided complete evidence that satisfies the entire criterion; ◕= Substantially meets—IRS provided evidence that satisfies a large portion of the criterion; ◑= Partially meets—IRS provided evidence that satisfies about half of the criterion; ◔= Minimally meets—IRS provided evidence that satisfies a small portion of the criterion; ○ = Does not meet—IRS provided no evidence that satisfies any of the criterion.

Source: GAO analysis of IRS February 2015 PPACA cost estimate (version 3). | GAO-15-624

APPENDIX VIII: COMMENTS FROM THE INTERNAL REVENUE SERVICE

DEPARTMENT OF THE TREASURY
INTERNAL REVENUE SERVICE
WASHINGTON, D.C. 20224

DEPUTY COMMISSIONER

June 12, 2015

Mr. James R. McTigue, Jr.
Director, Tax Issues
U.S. Government Accountability Office
441 G Street, N.W.
Washington, DC 20548

Dear Mr. McTigue:

Thank you for the opportunity to review the draft GAO report, IRS 2016 BUDGET: IRS Is Scaling Back Activities and Using Budget Flexibilities to Absorb Funding Cuts (GAO-15-624). We are pleased the GAO recognizes the significant funding reductions we have experienced since fiscal year 2010 and the impact those reductions have had on our staffing and performance as well as the steps that we have taken in recent years to reduce spending.

Below are the IRS's comments on each specific recommendation.

Recommendation #1: Implement internal controls to ensure the accuracy of information on major information technology investments reported in the annual congressional justification, such as obligations data.

Comment:
We agree with this recommendation. In addition to addressing this specific recommendation around accuracy in obligations data, we are taking a more holistic approach to address the issue. We are leveraging the expertise of staff throughout the Service and all of our available resources, to the extent possible, to conduct a comprehensive review of our capital planning and investment control (CPIC) activities, with particular emphasis on investment controls. The review will take into consideration current guidance governing the process and controls and will focus on our people resources, processes, and technology currently in place. We believe this comprehensive review by a multi-functional team will provide valuable recommendations for improvement and opportunities for more maturity in this area.

Recommendation #2: To the extent possible, report information about major information technology investments in the congressional justification in accordance with the standard terms published by the Comptroller General in the Budget Glossary (GAO 05-734SP).

Comment:
We agree with this recommendation. As part of our comprehensive review of our CPIC activities, any gaps in the use of standard terms will be identified and recommendations for changing to standard terms or improvements will be implemented.

Recommendation #3: When using key terms that are not defined in the Budget Glossary or in OMB guidance or when using a modification of these terms, provide definitions of key terms used to report information about major information technology investments in the congressional justification.

Comment:
We agree with this recommendation. As part of our comprehensive review of our CPIC activities, any gaps in the use of key terms will be identified and if we find any terms that are not defined in the Budget Glossary, we will provide the definitions of those terms.

If you have any questions, please contact me, or a member of your staff may contact Jeffrey V. Zottola, Associate Chief Financial Officer for Corporate Budget, at (202) 317-4038.

Sincerely,

J. Stuart Burns
Acting Deputy Commissioner for
Operations Support

End Notes

[1] GAO, Internal Revenue Service: Observations on IRS's Operations, Planning, and Resources, GAO-15-420R (Washington, D.C.: Feb. 27, 2015).

[2] All numbers presented in this report are nominal and not adjusted for inflation unless otherwise noted.

[3] GAO, Standards for Internal Control in the Federal Government, GAO/AIMD-00-21.3.1 (Washington, D.C.: Nov. 1999). We updated the Standards for Internal Control in the Federal Government in September 2014. The revised standards will be effective beginning in fiscal year 2016.

[4] Pub. L. No. 111-148, 124 Stat. 119 (Mar. 23, 2010), as amended by the Health Care and Education Reconciliation Act of 2010, Pub. L. No. 111-152, 124 Stat. 1029 (Mar. 30, 2010), which we refer to collectively as PPACA. IRS refers to PPACA by the acronym for the Affordable Care Act, ACA.

[5] GAO, GAO Cost Estimating and Assessment Guide: Best Practices for Developing and Managing Capital Program Costs, GAO-09-3SP (Washington, D.C.: March 2009).

[6] In addition to the amount appropriated to these four accounts, IRS supplements its budgetary resources through collections, such as reimbursables and user fees, which are not appropriated annually.

[7] Reprogramming shifts funds within an appropriation account and agencies may reprogram without additional statutory authority. IRS is restricted from reprogramming funds within appropriation accounts without committee approval if the reprogramming will, among other

things, augment existing programs, projects, or activities (which IRS refers to as budget activities) in excess of $5 million or 10 percent, whichever is less.

[8] Subject to committee approval, IRS was authorized in fiscal year 2015 to transfer up to 5 percent of appropriated funds across accounts.

[9] For fiscal year 1995 and thereafter, IRS was granted authority to retain new or increased fee receipts to supplement its annual appropriation. Pub. L. No. 103-329, title I, § 3, 108 Stat. 2382 (Sept. 30, 1994), as amended by Pub. L. No. 109-115, div. A, title II, § 209, 119 Stat. 2396 (Nov. 30, 2005). IRS retains only those user fees that were implemented after Sept. 30, 1994, or the portion of the fee that has been increased since Sept. 30, 1994, for those fees that were in effect prior to that date. For example, fees for installment agreements were established after Sept. 30, 1994, and therefore IRS retains the full amount of the fee collected. However, the fee for enrolling as an actuary is divided between IRS and the General Fund of the Treasury because this user fee existed when the grant of authority to retain certain user fees under Pub. L. No. 103-329 was enacted. See GAO-12-193 for more information on IRS user fees.

[10] Department of Treasury guidance defines a major investment as one that costs $10 million in either the current year or budget year, costs $50 million over the 5-year period extending from the prior year through two years after the budget year, or meets other specific criteria established by Treasury or OMB, such as having significant program or policy implications. OMB has instructed agencies not to categorize IT capital planning and Chief Information Officer function investments as major IT investments.

[11] See appendix I for more information on how IRS's budget and FTEs have changed since fiscal year 2009.

[12] From fiscal year 2010 through 2014, IRS did not have significant organizational changes or changes to the structure of its accounting system that could result in changes to obligations. The two fund centers that did not experience a decline between fiscal year 2010 and 2014 include: Chief Financial Officer and Executive Leadership and Direction. Privacy, Governmental Liaison and Disclosure was not established in fiscal year 2010; therefore, a percent change was not calculated.

[13] See appendix II for the non-interactive version of figure 1.

[14] 5 C.F.R. § 731.106(d)(1).

[15] See GAO, IRS 2015 Budget: Long-Term Strategy and Return on Investment Data Needed to Better Manage Budget Uncertainty and Set Priorities, GAO-14-605 (Washington, D.C.: June 12, 2014), in which we recommended that IRS develop a longterm strategy to address operations amidst an uncertain budget environment.

[16] In March 2015, the name changed from the Planning, Programming, and Audit Oversight office to the Planning, Programming, and Audit Coordination office.

[17] An obligation is defined as "A definite commitment that creates a legal liability of the government for the payment of goods and services ordered or received, or a legal duty on the part of the United States that could mature into a legal liability by virtue of actions on the part of the other party beyond the control of the United States." GAO, A Glossary of Terms Used in the Federal Budget Process, GAO-05-734SP (Washington, D.C.: September 2005).

[18] GAO, IRS 2014 Budget: Improvements Made to Budget Request and Cost Estimate, but Further Actions Needed, GAO-13-835 (Washington, D.C.: Sept. 26, 2013).

[19] GAO, Standards for Internal Control in the Federal Government, GAO/AIMD-00-21.3.1 (Washington, D.C.: November 1999).

[20] 31 U.S.C. § 1112(d).

[21] GAO-05-734SP, 64.

[22] Office of Management and Budget, Capital Programming Guide: Supplement to Circular A-11 (Washington, D.C.: Nov. 25, 2014).

[23] GAO, Tax Administration: IRS Needs to Further Refine Its Tax Filing Season Performance Measures, GAO-03-143 (Washington, D.C.: Nov. 22, 2002).

[24] The term 'useful life' has an established meaning in the field of accounting, where it is used for the purposes of calculating depreciation and is defined as the "typical operating service life of an asset for the purpose it was acquired."

[25] See GAO-14-605. For related recommendations, see Tax Gap: IRS Could Significantly Increase Revenue by Better Targeting Enforcement Resources, GAO-13-151; (Washington, D.C.: Dec. 5, 2012).

[26] See GAO-14-605.

[27] In GAO-13-835, we found that the cost estimate was not fully adjusted for inflation and so reported the nominal estimate, not adjusted for inflation.

[28] See GAO-09-3SP.

[29] See GAO-13-835. We did not review version 2 of the PPACA cost estimate because its release was delayed and the more current version 3 cost estimate was available.

In: IRS Budgets
Editor: Nicolas B. Cunningham
ISBN: 978-1-63484-466-6

Chapter 2

IRS 2015 Budget: Long-Term Strategy and Return on Investment Data Needed to Better Manage Budget Uncertainty and Set Priorities*

United States Government Accountability Office

Why GAO Did This Study

The financing of the federal government depends largely upon the IRS's ability to collect taxes, including providing taxpayer services that make voluntary compliance easier and enforcing tax laws to ensure compliance with tax responsibilities. For fiscal year 2015, the President requested a $12.5 billion budget for IRS, a 10.5 percent increase over the fiscal year 2014 budget.

Because of the size of IRS's budget and the importance of its service and compliance programs for all taxpayers, GAO was asked to review the fiscal year 2015 budget request for IRS. (In April 2014, GAO reported interim information on IRS's budget.) Among other things, this report assesses IRS's (1) strategy to address budget cuts and (2) use of ROI analysis. To conduct this work, GAO reviewed the fiscal year 2015 budget justification, IRS and OMB budget guidance, and IRS workload and performance data from fiscal years

* This is an edited, reformatted and augmented version of a United States Government Accountability Office publication, No. GAO-14-605, dated June 2014.

2009 to 2015. GAO also interviewed IRS officials and the National Taxpayer Advocate.

What GAO Recommends

GAO recommends that IRS (1) develop a long-term strategy to manage uncertain budgets, and (2) calculate actual ROI for implemented initiatives, compare actual ROI to projected ROI, and use the data to inform resource decisions. IRS agreed with GAO's recommendations, noting that it initiated a review of its base budget to ensure resources are aligned with its strategic plan and ROI is one of several factors relevant to making resource allocation decisions.

What GAO Found

Since fiscal year 2010, the Internal Revenue Service (IRS) budget has declined by about $900 million. As a result, funding is below fiscal year 2009 levels.

Staffing has also declined by about 10,000 full-time equivalents since fiscal year 2010, and performance has been uneven. For example, between fiscal years 2009 and 2013, the percentage of callers seeking live assistance and receiving it fluctuated between 61 percent and 74 percent. IRS took some steps to address budget cuts, such as reduced travel and training.

IRS's strategic plan does not address managing budget uncertainty, although there are several indicators that funding will be constrained for the foreseeable future. For example, in May 2014, the Office of Management and Budget (OMB) generally required a 2 percent reduction in agencies' fiscal year 2016 budget submission. OMB guidance also requires agencies to develop strategies for operating in an uncertain budget environment. According to IRS, extensive senior leadership turnover has contributed to the lack of a long-term strategy. Without a strategy, IRS may not be able to operate effectively and efficiently in an uncertain budget environment.

For fiscal year 2015, IRS calculated projected return on investment (ROI) for most of its enforcement initiatives. However, due to limitations—such as estimating the indirect effect coverage has on voluntary compliance—IRS does not calculate actual ROI or use it for resource decisions. These limitations are important, which is why GAO recommended in 2012 that IRS explore developing such estimates. Given that these limitations could take time to address, GAO demonstrated how IRS could use existing ROI data to review disparities across different enforcement programs to inform resource allocation decisions. Comparing projected and actual ROI is consistent with OMB guidance. While not the only factor in making resource decisions, actual ROI could provide useful insights on the productivity of a program.

ABBREVIATIONS

BCA	Budget Control Act of 2011
CI	Criminal Investigations
HIRIF	Health Insurance Reform Implementation Fund
FATCA	Foreign Account Tax Compliance Act
FTE	Full-time equivalent
IRDM	Information Reporting and Document Matching
IT	Information Technology
IRS	Internal Revenue Service
LB&I	Large Business and International Division
NTA	National Taxpayer Advocate
OMB	Office of Management and Budget
PPACA	Patient Protection and Affordable Care Act
PPA	Programs, projects, or activities
RAS	Research, Analysis, and Statistics Division
ROI	Return on investment
RRP	Return Review Program
SB/SE	Small Business/Self Employed Division
TIGTA	Treasury Inspector General for Tax Administration
W&I	Wage and Investment Division

* * *

June 12, 2014

The Honorable Tom Udall
Chairman
The Honorable Mike Johanns
Ranking Member

Subcommittee on Financial Services and General Government
Committee on Appropriations
United States Senate

The Honorable Charles W. Boustany, Jr.
Chairman
The Honorable John Lewis
Ranking Member
Subcommittee on Oversight
Committee on Ways and Means
House of Representatives

The financing of the federal government depends largely upon the Internal Revenue Service's (IRS) ability to collect taxes, including providing taxpayers with services to make voluntary compliance easier and enforcing tax laws to ensure compliance with tax responsibilities. For fiscal year 2015, the President requested $12.5 billion for IRS. This is an increase of 10.5 percent ($1.2 billion) over the fiscal year 2014 appropriation. In April 2014, we reported that IRS has absorbed approximately $900 million in budget cuts since fiscal year 2010.[1] In that interim report, we found the cuts resulted in significant staffing declines and uneven performance. For example, we reported that IRS staffing has been reduced by about 8,000 full-time equivalents (FTE) since fiscal year 2009. We also reported that while IRS provided a 67 percent level of telephone services for fiscal year 2014 through March 15, 2014 compared to 61 percent for the prior entire fiscal year, average wait times to reach a telephone assistor had almost doubled since fiscal year 2009—from 8.8 minutes to 16.8 minutes as of mid-March 2014.[2]

Because of the size of IRS's budget and the importance of its service and compliance programs for all taxpayers, you asked us to review the fiscal year 2015 budget request for IRS. In this report we (1) assess IRS's strategy to address the budget cuts, including sequestration; (2) assess any new use of return on investment (ROI) analysis; (3) summarize requested funding and actual and planned spending for the Patient Protection and Affordable Care Act (PPACA),[3] and assess the updated PPACA information technology (IT) cost estimate; and (4) describe IRS's progress in implementing open GAO budget-related recommendations and list any GAO open matters for Congress and recommendations for executive action that could result in potential savings or increased revenue for IRS.

To conduct our work for all objectives, we reviewed key documents—such as the fiscal year 2015 congressional justification for IRS—and interviewed IRS officials. For the first objective, we also analyzed IRS data, including FTE and performance data for key IRS operations; reviewed executive orders, and Office of Management and Budget (OMB) guidance on improving government performance and efficiency; and interviewed the National Taxpayer Advocate. For the second objective, we reviewed IRS and OMB guidance, and interviewed officials from the IRS Office of Corporate Budget and its Research, Analysis, and Statistics (RAS) Division. For the third objective, we summarized PPACA information by funding source since inception and analyzed new information on actual and planned spending for fiscal year 2014. We could not assess the updates to the PPACA cost estimate because the updated September 2013 cost estimate is still under review.[4] For the fourth objective, we obtained information on our open recommendations from various IRS officials and analyzed relevant documentation to determine if the recommendations were implemented. We spoke with IRS officials and reviewed data collection procedures and determined that the data used in this report were sufficiently reliable for our purposes. For further details on our scope and methodology, see appendix I.

We conducted this performance audit from November 2013 to June 2014 in accordance with generally accepted government auditing standards. Those standards require that we plan and perform the audit to obtain sufficient, appropriate evidence to provide a reasonable basis for our findings and conclusions based on our audit objectives. We believe that the evidence obtained provides a reasonable basis for our findings and conclusions based on our audit objectives.

BACKGROUND

IRS Budget Presentation

The congressional budget justification for IRS presents funding and FTE information at two levels: (1) appropriation account and (2) budget activity. In addition, it provides descriptions of program activities within each budget activity. IRS has four appropriation accounts:

- **Enforcement**. This account provides funding for the examination of tax returns, both domestic and international; administrative and judicial settlement of taxpayer appeals of examination findings; technical rulings; monitoring of employee pension plans; determination of qualifications of organizations seeking tax-exempt status; examination of tax returns of exempt organizations; enforcement of statutes relating to detection and investigation of criminal violations of the internal revenue laws; identification of underreporting of tax obligations; securing of unfiled tax returns; and collecting unpaid accounts.

- **Operations Support**. This account provides funding for overall planning, direction, and support for the IRS, including shared service support related to facilities services, rent payments, printing, postage, and security. This appropriation funds headquarters policy and management activities such as corporate support for strategic planning; communications and liaison; finance; human resources; equity, diversity and inclusion; research and statistics of income; and necessary expenses for information systems and telecommunication support, including development, security, and maintenance of IRS information systems.
- **Taxpayer Services**. This account provides funding for taxpayer service activities and programs. This includes printing forms and publications, processing tax returns and related documents, offering filing and account services, ensuring the availability of taxpayer assistance, and providing taxpayer advocacy services.
- **Business Systems Modernization**. This account provides resources for the planning and capital asset acquisition of IT to modernize the IRS business systems.

Budget activities divide appropriation accounts into additional functions. For example, the Enforcement appropriation is broken into three budget activities: Investigations, Exam and Collections, and Regulatory. Each budget activity, in turn, has multiple program activities. For example, Exam and Collections has 18 program activities.

The congressional justification presents how budget resources could be allocated to appropriation accounts. IRS is restricted from reprogramming funds within appropriation accounts without committee approval if the reprogramming will augment existing programs, projects, or activities (PPA) in excess of $5 million or 10 percent, whichever is less.[5] IRS refers to its PPAs as "budget activities." IRS generally notifies Congress if it expects to reprogram funds from one budget activity to another.

However, IRS is not restricted from shifting resources between program activities, which are activities within a budget activity and not subject to reprogramming restrictions. Further, while IRS cannot transfer resources from one appropriation account to another without specific statutory authority to do so, IRS could shift resources between any of the 18 program activities within the Exam and Collection budget activity without Congressional approval or notification.

Within the congressional justification, IRS also details its strategic goals and objectives for the agency. According to the fiscal year 2015 congressional justification for IRS, the IRS strategic plan guides program and budget decisions and supports the Department of the Treasury *Fiscal Year 2014 to 2017 Strategic Plan* and the Agency Priority Goal of expanding the availability and improving the quality of customer service options.

The congressional justification also details information on requested program increases (new program initiatives). The information includes why the funds are needed, how they will be used, and the number of staff by position needed to do the work. Some of the new program initiatives also include projected return on investment (ROI) calculations—the projected additional revenue collected, divided by the projected cost. For IRS, projected ROI is an estimate of how the agency expects a program initiative to perform. IRS defines three types of ROI:

- **Revenue producing**. The initiative yields direct, measureable results through enforcement activities.
- **Revenue protecting**. The initiative prevents the issuance of fraudulent refunds to persons posing as a taxpayer and resolves issues prior to issuing a refund.
- **Revenue enhancing**. The initiative leads to improved revenue collection through improvements in case selection, issue identification, and enforcement case treatment.

In recent years, some of the new program initiatives have been predicated on a program integrity cap adjustment. Congress passes these adjustments to allow additional funding above discretionary spending limits for certain activities that are expected to generate benefits that exceed cost. Of the 22 initiatives in the IRS fiscal year 2015 budget request, 17 are predicated on a program integrity cap adjustment.

Implementation of Major New Laws

IRS continues to implement four major new laws passed in recent years:

- **PPACA**. This law reforms the private insurance market and expands health coverage to the uninsured. IRS is responsible for implementing new provisions including new taxes, tax credits, and information reporting requirements.
- **Merchant card reporting**. This law requires payment settlement entities (e.g., banks) to report fiscal year information and the gross amount of reportable payment transactions (i.e., payment card and third party network transactions) to IRS.[6]
- **Cost basis reporting**. This law requires investment brokers to report the adjusted cost basis for certain publicly traded securities and whether a gain or loss is short or long-term.[7]
- **Foreign Account Tax Compliance Act (FATCA)**. This law adds reporting and other requirements relating to income from assets held abroad by: (1) requiring foreign financial and nonfinancial institutions to withhold 30 percent of payments made to such institutions by U.S. individuals, unless such institutions agree to disclose the identity of such individuals and report on their bank transactions, and (2) denying a tax deduction for interest on non-registered bonds issued outside the United States.[8]

IRS Has Taken Some Steps to Address Declining Budgets in the Short-Term, but Lacks a Long-Term Strategy

IRS Has Absorbed Substantial Budget Cuts in Recent Years

IRS's appropriations have ranged from a low of $10.2 billion in fiscal year 2005 to a high of $12.1 billion in fiscal year 2010. The fiscal year 2010 high was in part a result of a program integrity cap adjustment of $890 million. As we have previously reported, IRS's budget declined approximately $900 million between fiscal years 2010 and 2014.[9] These cuts reduced IRS's budget to below fiscal year 2009 funding levels. The largest budget reduction ($618 million) occurred in fiscal year 2013 because of sequestration ($594 million) and a 0.2 percent rescission ($24 million).[10] In fiscal year 2014, IRS's budget remained essentially flat, with an increase of $92 million for the improvement of identification and prevention of refund fraud and identity theft, and international and offshore compliance issues.[11] For fiscal year 2015, the President requested $12.5 billion for IRS, an increase of 10.5 percent ($1.2 billion) over fiscal year 2014 appropriations. See figure 1.

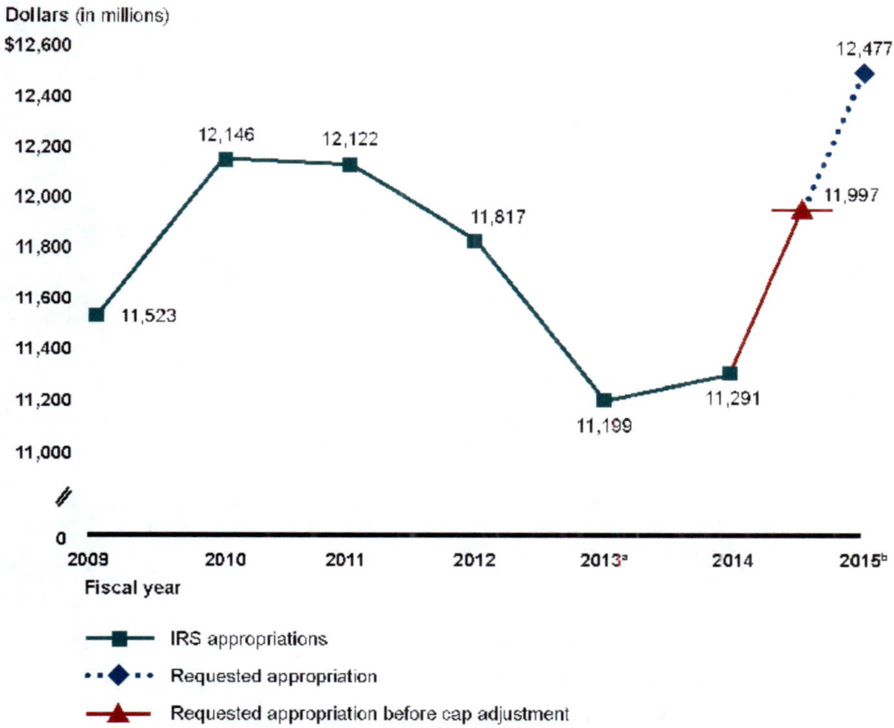

Source: GAO analysis of fiscal years 2009 through 2015 congressional justifications for IRS.

Notes: Amounts shown do not include other budgetary resources, such as user fees.

[a]Fiscal year 2013 levels represent an across-the-board rescission and reductions required by sequestration.

[b]For the fiscal year 2015 request, about $480 million, roughly 40 percent of the requested increase, is predicated on a program integrity cap adjustment, meaning Congress must approve funding above the discretionary spending limit.

Figure 1. IRS Appropriations, Fiscal Years 2009 through 2014, and Fiscal Year 2015 Request.

Staffing declined by more than 10,000 FTEs between fiscal years 2010 and 2014, which reduced IRS's total FTEs to below fiscal year 2009 levels. For fiscal year 2015, the President requested an increase of about 7,000 FTEs over fiscal year 2014, which would bring IRS above fiscal year 2012 levels. See figure 2.

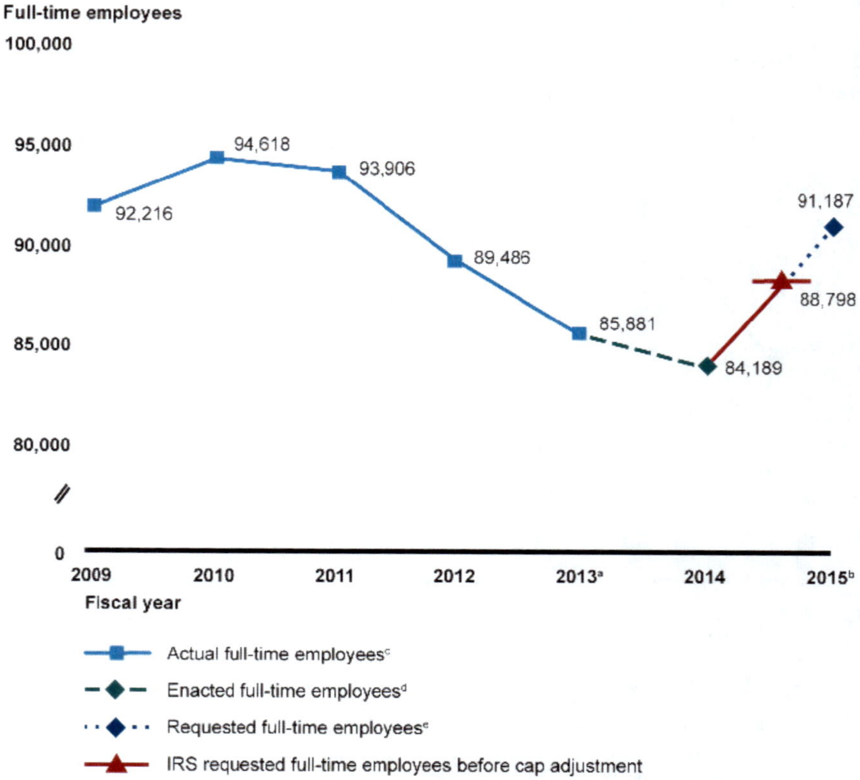

Source: GAO analysis of fiscal years 2009 through 2015 congressional justifications for IRS.

Notes: Amounts shown do not include FTEs funded with other budgetary resources, such as user fees.

[a]Fiscal year 2013 levels represent the across-the-board rescission and reductions required by sequestration.

[b]For the fiscal year 2015 request, about 2,400 FTEs (roughly 34 percent of the requested increase) are predicated on a program integrity cap adjustment, meaning Congress must approve funding above the discretionary spending limit. The cost of the fiscal year 2015 initiatives was estimated based on a January 1 hire date for most FTEs.

[c]Actual FTEs represent the total number of hours worked divided by the number of compensable hours applicable to each fiscal year. For example, in fiscal year 2013, there were 2,080 compensable hours.
[d]Enacted FTEs represent the number of FTEs provided for in the enacted budget.
[e]Requested FTEs is the number of FTEs requested in the President's Budget for IRS.

Figure 2. IRS Full-Time Equivalents Funded through Appropriations, Fiscal Years 2009 through 2013 (Actual), 2014 (Enacted), and 2015 (Requested).

IRS Performance Declined in Some Areas

Amidst these budget reductions, IRS's performance has declined in Enforcement and Taxpayer Services. IRS officials anticipate continued declines in fiscal year 2015. As shown in figure 3, IRS lowered its return examination and collection coverage targets. For example, the original audit coverage target for individual examinations was 1 percent for fiscal year 2014, but was lowered to 0.8 percent in the fiscal year 2015 congressional justification.

IRS's performance in assisting taxpayers has also suffered, including telephone and correspondence services. Between fiscal years 2009 and 2013, telephone level of service—the percentage of callers seeking live assistance and receiving it—fluctuated between 61 percent and 74 percent. As of April 19, 2014, after the filing season ended, fiscal year 2014 telephone level of service was 67 percent.[12] In addition, the average amount of time a taxpayer had to wait to talk to a telephone assistor increased since fiscal year 2009—from 8.8 minutes to 17.0 minutes, as of April 19, 2014. Moreover, from fiscal years 2009 through 2013, overage correspondence—paper correspondence to which IRS has not responded within 45 days of receipt—increased from 25 percent to 47 percent.[13] However, according to IRS, the 2014 filing season was relatively smooth, which IRS attributes to reduced call volume and fewer tax law changes.

IRS attributes performance declines to sequestration and furloughs. For example, the number of individual, high-income, and business return audits fell from fiscal year 2012 to 2013 because fewer staff were available to conduct audits. Similarly, reports by the IRS Oversight Board and the National Taxpayer Advocate (NTA) attribute performance declines in part to reduced funding.[14]

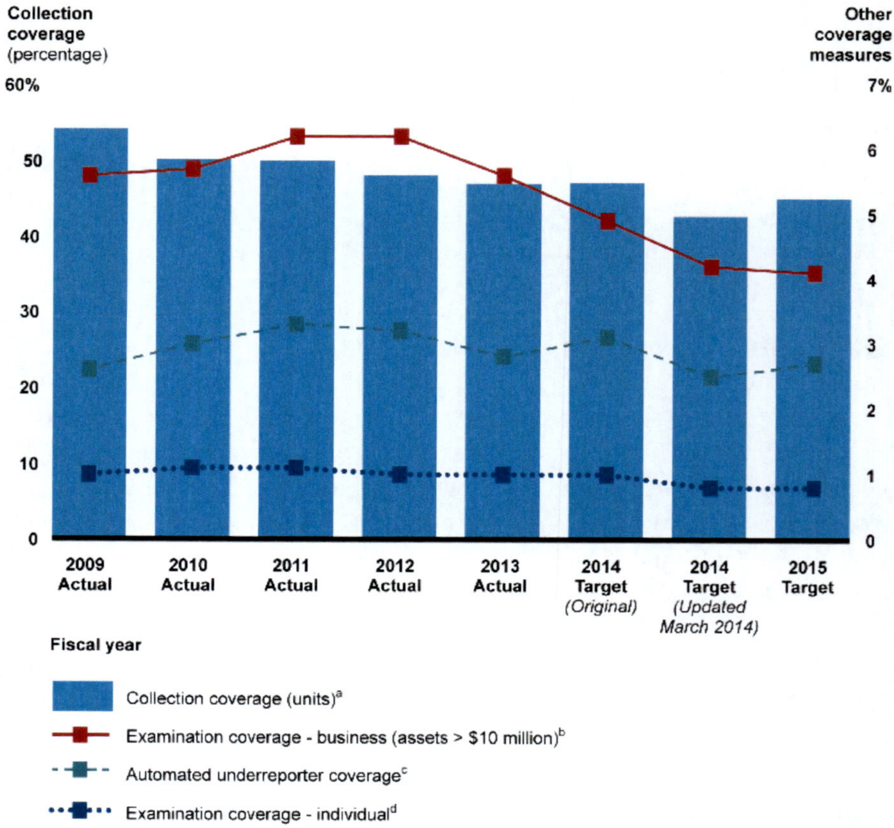

Source: GAO analysis of fiscal years 2009 through 2015 congressional justifications for IRS.

Notes:

[a]Collection coverage is the volume of collection work disposed, compared to the volume of collection work available.

[b]Examination coverage-business (assets > $10 million) is the number of Large Business and International (LB&I) division returns (C and S Corporations with assets over $10 million and all partnerships) examined and closed by LB&I during the current fiscal year, divided by the number of filings for the preceding calendar year.

[c]Automated underreporter coverage is a percentage representing the total number of Wage and Investment (W&I) division and Small Business/Self Employed (SB/SE) division contact closures (a closure resulting from a case where SB/SE and W&I made contact with a taxpayer), divided by the total return filings for the prior year.

[d]Examination coverage-individual is the sum of all individual Form 1040 returns closed by SB/SE, W&I, Tax Exempt and Government Entities and LB&I (Field

Exam and Correspondence Exam programs) divisions, divided by the total individual return filings for the prior calendar year.

Figure 3. IRS Return Examination and Collection Coverage Measures, Fiscal Years 2009 through 2013 (Actual) and 2014 and 2015 (Target).

IRS Faces an Increased Demand for Some Services

As staffing fell, IRS's workload increased in some areas as a result of statutory mandates and priority programs. For fiscal year 2014, IRS allocated 9 percent of its FTEs to these mandates and programs, including those to implement four new laws—PPACA, merchant card reporting, cost basis reporting, and FATCA. In addition, because instances of identity theft are more frequent, IRS has significantly increased resources devoted to refund fraud, which includes identity theft.

Since IRS began tracking refund fraud in fiscal year 2011, it has more than quadrupled the numbers of FTEs allocated to refund fraud, from 1,018 in fiscal year 2011 to 4,146 FTEs in fiscal year 2014 (about 5 percent of its total workforce). Table 1 shows the shift in FTEs to legislative mandates and priority programs.

Table 1. Full-Time Equivalents Allocated to Implement New Laws and Priority Programs, Fiscal Years 2009 through 2013 (Actual), 2014 (Enacted), and 2015 (Requested)

Statutory mandates and priority programs	FY 2009[a] actual	FY 2010[a] actual	FY 2011[a] actual	FY 2012[a] actual	FY 2013[a] actual	FY 2014[b] enacted	FY 2015[c] requested
Refund Fraud, Prevention Program (including identity theft)	–[d]	–[d]	1,018	3,299	4,146	4,146	4,603
International and Offshore Tax Administration	248	836	2,056	1,987	2,135	1,819	2,151
Patient Protection and Affordable Care Act	N/A	31	577	664	701	1,220	2,046
Merchant Card/Cost Basis Reporting	3	35	85	86	90	128	450
Foreign Account Tax Compliance Act	N/A	N/A	1	20	40	50	394

Table 1. (Continued)

Statutory mandates and priority programs	FY 2009[a] actual	FY 2010[a] actual	FY 2011[a] actual	FY 2012[a] actual	FY 2013[a] actual	FY 2014[b] enacted	FY 2015[c] requested
Return Preparer Oversight (includes Office of Professional Responsibility)	43	44	46	166	167	80	186
Return Review Program/Electronic Fraud Detection System	25	44	53	62	104	137	137
Total FTEs	319	990	3,836	6,284	7,383	7,580	9,967

Legend: FY = fiscal year; N/A = not applicable.

Source: IRS Office of Corporate Budget.

Notes:

[a]Actual FTEs represent the total number of hours worked based on IRS payroll data, divided by the number of compensable hours applicable to each fiscal year. For example, in fiscal year 2013, there were 2,080 compensable hours.

[b]Enacted FTEs represent the number of FTEs provided for the enacted budget.

[c]Requested FTEs represents the number of FTEs requested in the President's Budget for IRS. [d]IRS did not track FTEs allocated to refund fraud.

IRS Has Taken Some Steps to Address Budget Cuts

To reduce spending to address sequestration and other budget cuts, IRS has taken steps that include the following key efforts:[15]

- **Staff attrition and furloughs.** IRS absorbed the majority of its budget cuts through staff attrition and furloughs. Of the $567 million in savings realized in fiscal year 2013, $311 million resulted from attrition, hiring freezes, and furloughs. IRS implemented an exception-only hiring freeze in December 2010. In fiscal year 2013 alone, FTEs decreased by more than 2.7 percent—2,978—from fiscal year 2012 as a result of attrition, according to IRS. Of these savings, IRS generated $88.5 million from 3 furlough days.[16]
- **Reduced travel and training**. IRS substantially reduced employee training and related travel. Since fiscal year 2010, IRS reduced training costs by 83 percent and training-related travel costs by 87 percent by limiting employee travel and training to mission-critical projects. From fiscal years 2009 through 2013, IRS reduced the

amount it spent per employee on training from $1,600 to $200, according to data provided by IRS. Reductions of this magnitude are not sustainable, according to IRS officials. For fiscal year 2013, IRS reported a savings of $56.2 million by reducing agency-wide, non-technical training and non-case related travel. IRS attributes the savings to a greater use of technology and deferral of some standard training. IRS noted that in fiscal year 2013 the training budget was cut so the funds would be available to minimize furlough days and thereby maintain service to taxpayers.

- **E-file savings**. It costs IRS much less to process electronic returns than paper returns. IRS reported receiving 3.5 million fewer paper returns in fiscal year 2013 and 4.2 million more electronically filed returns, compared to fiscal year 2012. According to the fiscal year 2015 congressional justification, IRS realized savings of $11 million and 209 FTEs in fiscal year 2013 as a result of these changes, which exceeded projected savings by $2.4 million and 32 FTEs.
- **Space reduction**. IRS reported it completed 89 projects in fiscal year 2013 to reduce the amount of physical space it uses. As a result, IRS will rent 557,779 fewer square feet, which will save $15.7 million in rent annually. Further, IRS approved 30 more such projects in fiscal year 2014, which IRS estimates will reduce its space needs by another 350,000 square feet, producing an additional savings of about $11.3 million annually.

In addition, to address budget cuts, IRS has taken steps that it anticipates will produce savings in fiscal years 2014 and 2015.

- **Telephone and walk-in services**. In fiscal year 2014, IRS reduced or eliminated certain telephone and walk-in services. These actions are consistent with our finding in December 2012 that IRS needed to dramatically revise its strategy for providing telephone and correspondence services, and that incremental efficiency gains would not be enough to reverse service declines.[17] Specifically, IRS
  - limited telephone assistance to only basic tax law questions during the filing season and reassigned assistors to work account-related inquiries;
  - launched the "Get Transcript" tool, which allows taxpayers to obtain a viewable and printable transcript on www.irs.gov, and redirected taxpayers to automated tools for additional guidance;

  - redirected refund-related inquiries to automated services and did not answer refund inquiries until 21 days after a tax return was filed electronically or 6 weeks after a return was filed by paper (unless the automated service directed the taxpayer to contact IRS);
  - limited access to the Practitioner Priority Services line to only those practitioners working tax account issues;
  - limited live assistance and redirected requests for domestic employer identification numbers to IRS's online tool; and
  - eliminated free return preparation and reduced other services at IRS's walk-in sites.
- **IT reductions**. In part because of a lack of funding, IRS put a hold on aspects of two major IT projects:
  - Information Reporting and Document Matching (IRDM). This program is intended to improve business taxpayer compliance by matching business information returns (e.g., Form 1099-K) with individual tax returns to detect potential income underreporting. According to IRS IT officials, during the hold IRS will determine the best case management tool to use to meet IRDM's program requirements. IRS plans to leverage an off-the-shelf solution, which IRS believes will be more cost effective than building one.
  - Return Review Program (RRP). When fully deployed, RRP is expected to make use of leading-edge technology to detect, resolve, and prevent fraud. IRS expects to complete a plan to move beyond the hold on RRP in the summer of 2014. Officials said the plan will help inform IRS's funding needs for RRP.

IRS Has No Long-Term Strategy to Address an Uncertain Budget Environment

IRS does not outline a framework for how it should operate in an uncertain budget environment in either its fiscal year 2009 through 2013 strategic plan or its fiscal year 2014 goals and objectives included in the fiscal year 2015 congressional justification for IRS. While IRS has taken steps in the short-term to address budget cuts (including sequestration)— such as exception-only hiring and reducing or eliminating some telephone and walk-in services—it does not have a strategy to operate in an uncertain budget environment over the long-term.

Further, we found that IRS absorbed the majority of cuts as a result of actions that were not part of a long-term strategy. According to officials from IRS's Office of Corporate Budget, IRS has absorbed the majority of cuts through attrition and, as a result, the programs that experienced the most attrition were the programs that absorbed the most cuts.[18] In fiscal years 2012 through 2013, IRS absorbed roughly $516 million through attrition, nearly $383 million from enforcement activities, according to data provided by IRS. Officials also noted IRS has taken large budget cuts over the last several years. As IRS continues to operate in an uncertain budget environment, it continues to examine and prioritize what it can cut and what it can postpone. According to the NTA, the budget cuts have caused IRS to operate in crisis mode—reacting to external changes and putting out fires. The NTA also stated that IRS has no overall, cohesive strategy to understand what kind of services it should be providing and when to eliminate a service.

In response to our questions about IRS's lack of a long-term strategy, officials noted that one key problem has been the extensive turnover in senior leadership across the agency. Nineteen of 46 members—over 40 percent—of IRS's Senior Executive Team were on-board on or after October 1, 2013, including the new IRS Commissioner, who took office in December 2013.[19] However, IRS began an extensive review of its base budget in April 2014 in order to collect detailed spending and performance information for each of its distinct programs. Once IRS completes this review, management plans to determine the proper funding levels for each program and how to realign existing resources.

While this is an important start, it may not be sufficient over the long term. There are a number of indications that funding is unlikely to soon return to the growing and high budget levels IRS experienced in fiscal years 2010 and 2011.[20] First, our work on the nation's long-term fiscal outlook shows that growth in spending for federal health care and retirement programs will place increasing pressure on discretionary spending.[21] Second, in May 2014, OMB generally required a 2 percent reduction in agencies' fiscal year 2016 budget submission.[22] Third, under the Budget Control Act of 2011 (BCA), sequestration of discretionary appropriations could occur in any fiscal year through 2021.[23] In addition, as shown in figure 4, for the past several fiscal years IRS has been appropriated less than it requested, with a difference of 13 percent in fiscal year 2014. Looking back over a 10-year horizon provides further evidence that funding levels provided in fiscal years 2010 and 2011 were an exception and that the recent decline might be viewed more as a return to normal. All of these factors indicate that it is increasingly important for agencies to have longterm plans to address uncertain budget environments.

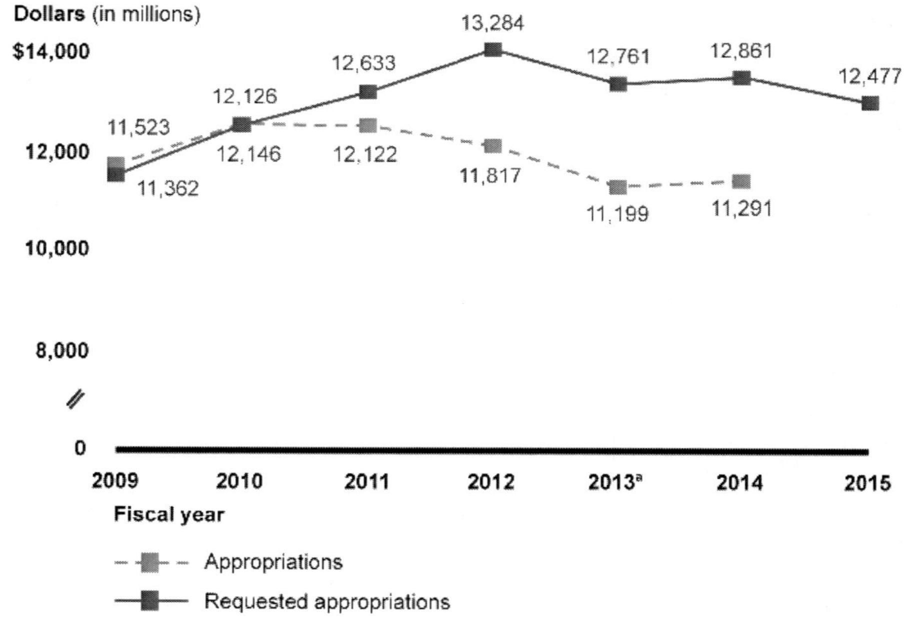

Source: GAO analysis of fiscal years 2009 through 2015 congressional justifications for IRS.

Notes: Amounts shown do not include other budgetary resources, such as user fees.

[a]Fiscal year 2013 levels represent an across-the-board rescission and reductions required by sequestration.

Figure 4. IRS Appropriations, Fiscal Years 2009 through 2014, and Requested Appropriations, Fiscal Years 2009 through 2015.

In addition, according to Executive Order No. 13576 and OMB guidance, agencies are to develop strategies for operating effectively and efficiently in an uncertain budget environment.[24] We have previously reported on steps that agencies can take to do this.[25] These include reexamining programs, related processes, and organizational structures to determine whether they are effectively or efficiently achieving their mission. They also include streamlining or consolidating management or operational processes and functions to make them more cost effective.[26]

We have also made recommendations to IRS on how it can more strategically manage operations in specific areas, such as developing a long-term strategy to improve its online services.[27]

A long-term strategy that includes a fundamental reexamination of IRS's operations, programs, and organizational structure could help it operate more effectively and efficiently in an environment of budget uncertainty. Although IRS has taken steps in the short term, they may not be sufficient to stem performance declines. While IRS was able to mitigate some of the effects of sequestration, it is unlikely that the steps taken are sustainable strategies in the long term. Moreover, the extent of turnover in senior leadership makes it even more important to have a long-term guiding strategy.

IRS Does Not Use Return on Investment Data to Evaluate the Performance of Revenue Initiatives or to Inform Enforcement Resource Allocation Decisions

IRS Calculates a Projected, but Not Actual, ROI for Most New Enforcement Initiatives

IRS calculates a projected return on investment (ROI)—the projected revenue divided by the projected cost—for most proposed new enforcement initiatives cited in the congressional justification.[28] In the calculation, revenue represents the expected direct revenue effects of the initiatives, but does not reflect any indirect revenue effects that may result if the added enforcement activities increase voluntary compliance among taxpayers. Cost includes all enforcement-related resources used by IRS, but does not incorporate compliance costs imposed on taxpayers.

For fiscal year 2015, IRS proposed 13 enforcement initiatives (see table 2). IRS estimated a projected ROI for 8 of the initiatives. In addition, 11 initiatives are predicated on funding from a program integrity cap adjustment. IRS calculates ROI over a 3-year period (based on projections of associated costs and expected revenue) because it expects that staff working on the initiative will reach their full performance after 3 years.

Table 2. Fiscal Year 2015 New Enforcement Initiatives

Enforcement initiative	Type of ROI initiative[a]	Full performance ROI (fiscal year 2017) (dollars)	Program integrity cap adjustment
Prevent Identity Theft and Refund Fraud		Revenue protecting	$22.4
Expand Audit Coverage	Revenue protecting	20.5	✓
	Revenue producing	7.1	✓
Address Impact of Patient Protection and Affordable Care Act (PPACA) Statutory Requirements		Revenue protecting	14.0
		Revenue producing	2.3
Expand Coverage of High Wealth Individuals and Enterprises	Revenue producing	11.3	✓
Enhance Collection Coverage	Revenue producing	8.5	✓
Improve Coverage of Partnerships and Flow-Through Entities	Revenue producing	6.8	✓
Address International and Offshore Compliance Issues	Revenue producing	4.8	✓
Leverage Data to Improve Case Selection	Revenue enhancing	2.0	✓
Build Out Tax Return Preparer Compliance and Professional Responsibility Activities	Strategic revenue producing	—	✓
Expand Compliance Coverage in the Tax-Exempt Sector	Strategic revenue producing	—	✓
Implement IT Changes to Deliver the Foreign Account Tax Compliance Act (FATCA)	Strategic revenue producing	—	✓

Enforcement initiative	Type of ROI initiative[a]	Full performance ROI (fiscal year 2017) (dollars)	Program integrity cap adjustment
Leverage Digital Evidence for Criminal Investigations (CI)	Strategic revenue producing	—	✓
Pursue Fraud Referrals, Employment Tax, and Abusive Tax Schemes	Strategic revenue producing	—	✓

Source: GAO analysis of fiscal year 2015 congressional justification for IRS.

[a]Revenue protecting means the initiative prevents the issuance of fraudulent returns to persons posing as a taxpayer and resolves issues prior to issuing a taxpayer's refund. Revenue producing means the initiative yields direct, measureable results through ROI enforcement activities. Revenue enhancing means the initiative improves technology by providing better case selection, issue identification, and enforcement case treatment. Strategic revenue producing means the initiative does not have immediately measurable ROI, but clear long-term revenue effects.

IRS Does Not Calculate an Actual ROI Once Initiatives Are Implemented

As of May 2014, IRS has not determined the extent to which the resources actually devoted to enforcement initiatives differ from the 3- year projections of resources described in prior budget justifications. Nor has IRS computed actual rates of return on the resources that were actually used for specific initiatives. As a result, neither IRS nor others know whether the program initiatives it proposed, once implemented, were as productive as expected. We have reported that calculating actual ROI would be a significant step forward in determining how initiatives are performing and whether calculations for projected ROIs need to be adjusted.[29] IRS, following a recommendation from the Treasury Inspector General for Tax Administration, is conducting a feasibility study to identify the necessary steps and challenges that exist to measure actual revenue for enforcement initiatives.[30] IRS expects to complete the study in December 2014.

IRS officials noted that one reason they do not calculate actual ROI for enforcement initiatives is because it is difficult to determine which staff have actually worked on a particular initiative over a multi-year period. According to IRS officials, IRS creates exam plans each year based on division goals and priority areas, which can change on an annual basis. As such, staff may be initially hired to work on a specific initiative, but may work on another initiative the following year. According to IRS officials, different individuals may work on an initiative during the course of a year, rather than specific individuals being dedicated to the initiative 100 percent of the time. When staff initially hired to work on an initiative are transferred to another initiative, there can be significant differences between the scope of the proposed and implemented versions of the initiative. In our prior work, we noted that if IRS falls behind on its hiring plans, staff may not reach their full potential as quickly as anticipated, which ultimately could delay projected revenue gains.[31]

In addition, officials from the IRS Corporate Budget Office cited difficulties in tracking ROI-related information on funded initiatives, because of difficulties in matching information between IRS systems for formulating and executing its budget. IRS has established funded program codes (previously known as internal order codes) as a mechanism to track specific initiatives—such as IRDM and merchant card/cost basis reporting—which could provide actual ROI, but IRS mainly uses these codes to track information that is of interest to congressional staff.

Comparing projected ROI to actual ROI is consistent with project management concepts, internal control standards, OMB guidance, and our prior work on performance management.[32] In addition, budget decision makers in Congress have stated that a comparison of projected ROI to actual ROI initiatives would be useful information to have. Until IRS calculates actual ROI for its implemented enforcement initiatives, it is not accountable for the ROI it projected when requesting funding.

IRS Calculates Actual ROI for Its Broad Enforcement Programs, but Does Not Use It to Inform Resource Decisions

In June 2009, we recommended that IRS calculate actual ROI because it provides information about how programs and initiatives are performing and the possible need to adjust ROI methodologies to more effectively project results of future proposed initiatives.[33] We have recognized that calculating actual ROI is challenging and existing data may not be complete.

Based on our prior recommendation, IRS began reporting actual ROI in the fiscal year 2014 congressional justification for the following three major enforcement programs:

- **Examination**. This program conducts examinations of tax returns of individual taxpayers, businesses, and other types of organizations to verify that the tax reported is correct.
- **Collection**. This program collects delinquent taxes and secures delinquent tax returns through the appropriate use of enforcement tools such as liens, levies, seizures of assets, installment agreements, offers in compromise, substitute for returns, and 26 U.S.C. § 6020(b), which allows the IRS to prepare returns if a taxpayer fails to file a return.
- **Automated Underreporter**. This program matches taxpayer information returns against data reported on individual tax returns and verifies the information to identify any discrepancies.

According to IRS officials, IRS calculates the actual ROI for these programs because total enforcement revenue collected is allocated to these three categories. IRS reports the actual ROI in the congressional justification, based on our previous recommendation and congressional budget decision makers' interest in this information. However, IRS does not use this actual ROI information for resource allocation decisions because the data do not reflect marginal ROI, nor do they include the indirect effects of IRS enforcement activities on voluntary compliance.[34] Moreover, because of the time required to work enforcement cases to completion, the costs associated with assessing and collecting additional revenues may be spread over more than one fiscal year and are not necessarily aligned with revenue collections that may occur in subsequent years. These limitations are critical concerns, which is why we recommended in 2012 that IRS develop estimates of marginal direct revenue and marginal direct costs within each enforcement program. We further recommended that IRS explore the potential of estimating the marginal influence of enforcement activity on voluntary compliance.[35] However, given that these data gaps could take considerable time to fill, we also demonstrated how IRS planners could in the meantime review actual (average) ROI across different enforcement programs and across different groups of cases within these programs to better inform resource allocation decisions. As we noted, the planners could consider this information in combination with their professional judgment relating to other relevant but currently unquantifiable factors. In fact, while limited in scope, we demonstrated how a hypothetical shift in resources could potentially increase direct revenue by $1 billion annually, without significant negative effects on voluntary compliance.

Table 3. Actual Return on Investment (ROI) for Major IRS Enforcement Programs (Dollars in Millions)

Enforcement program	Fiscal year 2010			Fiscal year 2011			Fiscal year 2012			Fiscal year 2013		
	Cost	Revenue	ROI	Cost	Revenue	ROI	Cost	Revenue	ROI	Cost	Revenue	ROI
Examination [a]	$4,371	$23,563	5.4	$4,333	$18,924	4.4	$4,232	$14,476	3.4	$3,965	$16,662	4.2
Collection	1,948	29,105	14.9	1,939	31,060	16.0	1,742	30,442	17.5	1,660	31,396	18.9
Automated Underreporter	262	4,924	18.8	270	5,245	19.4	267	5,269	19.7	258	5,287	20.5
Total	$6,581	$57,592	8.8	$6,543	$55,229	8.4	$6,242	$50,187	8.0	$5,883	$53,345	9.1

Source: Fiscal year 2015 congressional justification for IRS.

Notes: Numbers may not add due to rounding.

[a] Revenues collected in a given year are not necessarily associated with costs realized in a given year because cases may cross years. Current revenue streams may be the result of past enforcement activity, such as installment agreements.

The development of data relating to marginal ROI would also enable IRS to improve its projections of ROI for enforcement initiatives, particularly those that expand coverage for specific taxpayer categories. IRS currently knows little about the extent to which marginal yields differ from average yields within specific return categories; consequently, it does not know the extent to which its ROI projections, which are based on average yields, may be overstated.[36] By collecting the data needed to compute actual ROI for expanded coverage enforcement initiatives, IRS would be able to determine whether marginal returns are significantly lower than average returns; thereby, IRS would have better information for deciding whether the expanded coverage should be maintained, cut back, or expanded further in future years. Actual productivity information and better ROI projections can also help budget decision makers in determining funding levels for IRS.

Since Inception, IRS Has Spent $859 Million to Implement PPACA, but an Updated IT Cost Estimate Is Unavailable for Review

When enacted, PPACA gave IRS responsibility for implementing a number of provisions. From fiscal year 2010 through 2012 and again in 2014, IRS received funds for PPACA implementation activities from the Department of Health and Human Services Health Insurance Reform Implementation Fund (HIRIF), which is used to fund the federal administrative expenses to implement PPACA. To implement PPACA provisions in fiscal years 2013 and 2014, IRS requested $360.5 million and $439.6 million, respectively, but it did not receive this funding. As we previously reported, of the $12.5 billion IRS requested for fiscal year 2015, $451.7 million is to implement PPACA.[37] Table 4 shows the amounts IRS obligated for PPACA implementation from fiscal years 2010 to 2014.

For fiscal year 2014, IRS identified seven initiatives related to PPACA implementation. Table 5 shows how much IRS plans to spend on these initiatives in fiscal year 2014 and the amount spent through the middle of fiscal year 2014. Of the total planned spending for fiscal year 2014— $400.6 million—IRS has obligated $87.1 million through March 31, 2014.

Table 4. Patient Protection and Affordable Care Act Spending, Fiscal Years 2010 to 2014 (in Millions)

	Fiscal years					
Appropriation account	**2010**	**2011**	**2012**	**2013**	**2014 (as of March 31)**	**Total**
Health Insurance Reform Implementation Fund	$20.7	$168.2	$299.2	-	$1.1	**$489.2**
Taxpayer Services	-	-	-	4.3	2.2	**6.5**
Enforcement	-	-	-	19.3	7.7	**27.0**
Operations Support	-	-	-	190.7	20.1	**210.8**
Operations Support User Fees	-	-	-	69.7	56.0	**125.7**
Total	**$20.7**	**$168.2**	**$299.2**	**$284.0**	**$87.1**	**$859.2**

Source: GAO analysis of IRS documents.

Note: Numbers may not add due to rounding.

Table 5. IRS Fiscal Year 2014 Planned and Actual Spending on Patient Protection and Affordable Care Act by Initiative (in Millions)

Initiative	Fiscal year 2014 planned spending	Fiscal year 2014 obligations as of March 31, 2014
Administer New Fees on Drug Manufacturers and Health Insurers	$2.3	$1.0
Promoting Compliance with Other New Provisions	8.5	3.1
Strengthen Oversight of Exempt Hospitals	3.0	1.6
Assist Taxpayers Understanding ACA Issues	23.7	2.2
Support of Implementation & Taxpayer Issues (Counsel, Appeals & TAS)	5.2	2.2
Applications Development/Systems Software/Contracts/Systems Testing & Delivery	344.5	71.4
Program Management, Business Design and Specifications and Oversight of Data Sharing of Federal Tax Information	13.4	5.5
Total	$400.6	$87.1

Source: GAO analysis of IRS documents.

Note: Numbers may not add due to rounding.

Table 6 shows how much IRS requested to implement PPACA initiatives in fiscal year 2015.

Table 6. Fiscal Year 2015 Budget Request for IRS to Implement the Patient Protection and Affordable Care Act (in Millions)

Initiative	Fiscal year 2015
Expand Telecom Infrastructure to Handle Increased Demand	$16.0
Improve Taxpayer Service and Return Processing	73.9
Address Impact of Affordable Care Act (ACA) Statutory Requirements	56.1
Implement Information Technology (IT) Changes to Deliver Tax Credits and Other Requirements	305.6
Total	$451.7

Source: GAO analysis of IRS documents.
Note: Numbers may not add due to rounding.

As of December 2012, IRS estimated the full life-cycle costs for PPACA to be $1.89 billion from fiscal years 2010 through 2026. According to IRS officials, an update to the December 2012 PPACA cost estimate was completed in September 2013. The updated cost estimate is still under review and it will not be released until January 2015. As a result, we cannot assess the progress made on implementing our prior recommendations.

In September 2013, we reported that IRS made progress in updating its initial October 2010 PPACA cost estimate, in accordance with best practices as identified in the GAO Cost Estimating and Assessment Guide.[38] However, we found that IRS could take further steps to improve the estimate's accuracy and credibility. At that time, IRS agreed with the majority of the actions we recommended. IRS officials reported that the September 2013 PPACA cost estimate does address some of the recommended actions. For example, IRS officials said they implemented our recommendation to document how cost drivers are selected for future sensitivity analyses. However, until the September 2013 cost estimate is available for our review, we cannot verify these changes.

IRS IMPLEMENTED THREE OF SEVEN PRIOR RECOMMENDATIONS

Since September 2013, IRS at least partially implemented three recommendations made in our prior reviews of its budget justification documents. Two of the implemented recommendations resulted in more transparent reporting and greater accessibility to IT investments data. Table 7 summarizes the recommendations implemented by IRS.

Table 7. Prior GAO Recommendations Implemented by IRS

Report	Recommendation	Action taken	Benefit
GAO-12-603	Modify funding request for new hires Prepare funding requests for new staff based on estimated hiring dates.	Partially implemented: IRS changed how it requests funding for some new hires in the President's fiscal year 2015 budget request; however, it still assumed a January 1 hire date for most new staff.	Aligning funding requests more closely with estimated costs, hiring plans or both would represent workforce needs more accurately and transparently.
GAO-13-835	Enhance transparency of PPACA investment data Publicly report ACA IT investment as a major investment on the OMB IT Dashboard and the fiscal year 2015 budget request, including standard cost, schedule, and performance information.	Fully implemented: IRS reported the ACA IT investment as a major investment in the fiscal year 2015 budget request and included an Exhibit 300 (a capital asset plan), which is publicly available on the OMB Dashboard.	Publicly reporting on IRS's ACA IT investment eases the monitoring ofimplementation and enhances transparency.

Report	Recommendation	Action taken	Benefit
GAO-13-835	Expand and consolidate information on major IT investments into justification materials Report key data on major IT investments in one consolidated document, such as the congressional justification, in consultation with congressional stakeholders.	Fully implemented: IRS included new, useful information on its major IT investments in its fiscal year 2015 budget request.	Consolidating key budget and performance information on major IT investments in one budget document (such as the congressional justification) ensures decision makers have comprehensive, easy to understandinformation on major IT investments.

Source: GAO analysis of prior GAO reports on IRS budget requests.

Four budget-related recommendations to IRS remain open. As shown in table 8, IRS is planning to implement two of the open recommendations, but only partially agrees with the two remaining open recommendations. Appendix II identifies all of our products with open matters for Congress and recommendations to IRS regarding tax administration that could result in potential savings or increased revenues.

Table 8. Budget-Related Recommendations to IRS that Remain Open

Report	Open recommendations	Benefit	Status
GAO-12-603	Conduct cost-effectiveness analyses Ensure cost-effectiveness analyses are conducted for future significant investments when	Without cost-effectiveness analyses, budget decision makers do not have information to compare alternatives and it may be difficult to	IRS stated it is taking steps to implement this recommendation.

Table 8. (Continued)

Report	Open recommendations	Benefit	Status
	there are alternative approaches for achieving a given benefit, such as for any new significant PPACA projects.	determine the best use of resources.	
GAO-12-603	Develop a quantitative measure of scope At a minimum, develop a quantitative measure of scope for its major IT investments, in order to have complete information on the performance of these investments.	A quantitative measure of scope is a good practice as it provides an objective measure of whether an investment delivered the functionality that was paid for.	In March 2014, IRS reported thatit has practices and processes inplace that address this recommendation, including quarterly reports to Congress and a baseline change request process. However, we do not believe these practices address our recommendation, as neither approach includes a quantitative measure. For this reason we believe the recommendation is still warranted.[a]
GAO-13-835	Improve budget formulation guidance	Expanding internal guidance for pre-selection budget formulation templates facilitates more complete	IRS is taking steps to implement this recommendation during fiscal year 2016 budget formulation.

Report	Open recommendations	Benefit	Status
	Improve guidance given to business units for the pre-selection budget formulation process, emphasizing the importance of information on the estimated impact—qualitative or quantitative—of proposed budget initiatives.	information for internal budget decision-making.	
GAO-13-835	Further refine updates to the PPACA cost estimate Improve the accuracy and credibility of future updates to the PPACA cost estimate by taking the following actions to more closely follow best practices outlined in the GAO Cost Guide: •Use earned value management to capture actual costs and use them as a basis for future updates.	Developing a cost estimate that meets additional best practices, will foster accountability, improve insight, and provide objective information.	IRS agreed with all of the actionsrecommended, except using earned value management and with validating the PPACA cost estimate by preparing a second, independent cost estimate, in part because of cost and burden.IRS officials reported that the other actions were implemented into version 2 of the PPACA cost estimate.

Table 8. (Continued)

Report	Open recommendations	Benefit	Status
	•Explain why variances occurred between the current estimate and previous estimates. •Document how cost drivers are selected for future sensitivity analyses. •Conduct future risk and uncertainty analyses consistent with best practices, and develop and document plans to address risks. •Validate the original cost estimate by preparing a second, independent cost estimate.		The updated cost estimate was completed in September 2013, and we plan to review it once it is released in January 2015.

Source: GAO analysis of prior GAO reports on IRS budget requests.

Note: [a]GAO, *Information Technology: IRS Needs to Improve the Reliability and Transparency of Reported Investment Information*, GAO-14-298 (Washington, D.C.: Apr. 2, 2014).

CONCLUSION

IRS is operating in an uncertain budget environment, and there are implications that significant funding increases are unlikely in the foreseeable future. While IRS has taken steps in recent years to reduce spending, those steps were generally reactionary. Now is the time to fundamentally reexamine its operations, programs, and organizational structure to determine how to most efficiently and effectively accomplish its mission. Creating such a roadmap will help ensure that IRS effectively provides taxpayers with services to make voluntary compliance easier and to enforce the tax laws, so that taxpayers fulfill their tax responsibilities. A roadmap will also help provide continuity in light of any future turnover among senior executives.

As IRS examines its operations, it will need multiple sources of data on which to base its assessment and to ultimately make resource allocation decisions. While not necessarily the only factor in making resource allocation decisions, actual ROI could provide insight on the productivity of a program and inform estimating techniques for new initiatives. In turn, better estimates of ROI and actual productivity information can help budget decision makers in determining funding levels for IRS. Comparing projected and actual ROIs can help hold managers and the IRS accountable for the funding received.

RECOMMENDATIONS FOR EXECUTIVE ACTION

We recommend the Commissioner of Internal Revenue take the following three actions:

As a result of turnover in IRS's Senior Executive Team and in order to enhance budget planning and improve decision making and accountability, we recommend IRS

- develop a long-term strategy to address operations amidst an uncertain budget environment. As part of the strategy, IRS should take steps to improve its efficiency, including (1) reexamining programs, related processes, and organizational structures to determine whether they are effectively and efficiently achieving the IRS mission, and (2) streamlining or consolidating management or operational processes and functions to make them more cost-effective.

Because ROI provides insights on the productivity of a program and is one important factor in making resource allocation decisions, we recommend IRS

- calculate actual ROI for implemented initiatives, compare the actual ROI to projected ROI, and provide the comparison to budget decision makers for initiatives where IRS allocated resources; and
- use actual ROI calculations as part of resource allocation decisions.

AGENCY COMMENTS AND OUR EVALUATION

We provided a draft of this report to the Commissioner of Internal Revenue for comment. In written comments, reproduced in appendix III, IRS agreed with our recommendations. Regarding our recommendation to develop a long-term strategy to address operations amidst an uncertain budget environment, IRS noted that it is conducting a review of its budget base to ensure resources are aligned with IRS Strategic Goals, Objectives, and Priorities, and will adjust its fiscal year 2015 budget as a result of this review. Regarding our ROI recommendations, IRS agreed that ROI is one of several factors relevant to making resource allocation decisions. However, IRS noted that determining the impact of an initiative will always rely on estimates, as the results of an initiative are the difference between actual results and what would have occurred in the absence of the initiative, which cannot be measured. We agree that projected benefits are based on estimates, but it is possible to develop an estimate for what would have occurred in the absence of the initiative. Moreover, this report emphasizes comparisons between projected and actual ROI, not comparing actual results with what would have occurred in the absence of an initiative. Comparing projected and actual ROI is important to assist budget decision makers in determining funding levels for IRS and to hold managers and the IRS accountable for the funding received. IRS also provided technical comments on our draft report, which we incorporated as appropriate.

James R. McTigue, Jr.
Director,
Tax Issues Strategic Issues

APPENDIX I: OBJECTIVES, SCOPE, AND METHODOLOGY

We were asked to review the President's fiscal year 2015 budget request for the Internal Revenue Service (IRS). The objectives of this report were to (1) assess IRS's strategy to address the budget cuts, including sequestration; (2) assess any new use of return on investment (ROI) analysis; (3) summarize requested funding and actual and planned spending for the Patient Protection and Affordable Care Act (PPACA)[1] and assess the updated PPACA information technology cost estimate; and (4) describe IRS's progress in implementing open GAO budget-related recommendations and list any GAO open matters for Congress and recommendations for executive action that could result in potential savings or increased revenue for IRS.

To assess IRS's strategy to address the budget cuts, including sequestration, we summarized IRS's budget, staffing, performance, and workload trends for fiscal years 2009 through 2015. We selected fiscal year 2009 as a starting point because fiscal year 2009 was the year prior to IRS's highest appropriation in recent years. To summarize these trends, we analyzed congressional justifications for IRS for fiscal years 2009 through 2015 and performance data for key IRS operations. When we describe full-time equivalent (FTE) trends, the actual number of FTEs represents total number of hours worked (or to be worked) divided by the number of compensable hours applicable to each fiscal year, according to definition provided by IRS. Enacted FTEs represents the number of FTEs provided for the enacted budget. Requested FTEs represents the number of FTEs requested in the President's Budget for IRS.

We also analyzed FTE and workload trends on IRS identified priority programs, which include new statutory mandates. We reviewed reports by the IRS Oversight Board, Treasury Inspector General for Taxpayer Administration (TIGTA), and the National Taxpayer Advocate (NTA), which provided some possible reasons for performance declines. In addition, we analyzed proposed program initiatives in the fiscal year 2015 congressional justification and determined which ones were predicated on a program integrity cap adjustment, which Congress passes to allow additional funding above discretionary spending limits. We also analyzed steps IRS has taken to address budget cuts, including sequestration. To analyze these steps, we reviewed the fiscal year 2015 congressional justification, including information on savings initiatives realized or proposed from fiscal years 2009 through 2015 and prior GAO work on sequestration. We also interviewed IRS officials in IRS offices of Corporate Budget and Information Technology and the NTA. We compared IRS efforts to address uncertain budgets to Executive Order 13576 "Delivering an Efficient, Effective, and Accountable Government" and Office of Management and Budget (OMB) guidance. In addition, we compared IRS efforts to leading practices in government performance and efficiency.

To assess any new use of ROI analysis, we reviewed the fiscal year 2015 congressional justification to identify IRS's projected and actual ROI; obtained data from IRS to determine the new initiatives by projected revenue, cost, and type; and summarized projected ROI by type for new enforcement initiatives and actual ROI for IRS's three enforcement programs—

Examination, Collection, and Automated Underreporter. As part of our analysis of proposed program initiatives, we also identified any new enforcement initiative predicated on a program integrity cap adjustment. We reviewed OMB and IRS guidance on new program initiatives and interviewed IRS Corporate Budget officials to determine how IRS calculates ROI for proposed initiatives and the extent to which it compares estimated ROI to actual ROI for funded new initiatives. We reviewed prior GAO and TIGTA reports to identify criteria for measuring actual revenue of new program initiatives and for use in resource allocation decisions. We also interviewed IRS Research, Analysis, and Statistics officials to discuss the IRS feasibility study on ROI calculations and challenges in calculating actual ROI for new enforcement initiatives, as well as current enforcement programs.

To provide funding and spending information on PPACA, we summarized data by appropriation account since program inception (fiscal year 2010) and analyzed new information on actual and planned spending for fiscal year 2014, based on congressional budget justifications for IRS and on spending plans. We could not assess the most recent update of the PPACA cost estimate—September 2013—because it is still under review.[2] However, to determine IRS's progress in updating its cost estimate (consistent with our recommendation in 2013 to follow best practices identified in the GAO Cost Estimating and Assessment Guide) we interviewed and obtained some documentation from IRS officials.

To describe IRS's progress in implementing our prior budget-related recommendations, we obtained information from various IRS officials and reviewed relevant documentation, including the fiscal year 2015 congressional budget justification and the IRS Joint Audit Management Enterprise System reports, which track IRS actions taken to implement GAO recommendations. We then determined which recommendations were implemented. We also searched the GAO Engagement Reporting System to identify prior GAO open matters for Congress and recommendations for executive action. We then identified whether the recommendation or matter could result in a potential savings, increased revenue, or indirect financial benefits for IRS.

We interviewed IRS officials and determined that the data presented in this report were sufficiently reliable for our purposes. We conducted our work in Washington, D.C., where key IRS officials involved with the budget are located.

We conducted this performance audit from November 2013 to June 2014 in accordance with generally accepted government auditing standards. Those standards require that we plan and perform the audit to obtain sufficient, appropriate evidence to provide a reasonable basis for our findings and conclusions based on our audit objectives. We believe that the evidence obtained provides a reasonable basis for our findings and conclusions based on our audit objectives.

APPENDIX II: GAO PRODUCTS WITH OPEN MATTERS FOR CONGRESS AND RECOMMENDATIONS TO THE INTERNAL REVENUE SERVICE (IRS)

In the 37 GAO products listed below, as of March 13, 2014, there are 10 open matters for Congress and 72 open recommendations to IRS. Of these matters and recommendations, 20 increase revenue, 15 increase savings, 10 increase both savings and revenue, and 37 have indirect financial benefits.

Table 9. List of Open Matters for Congress and Recommendations to IRS That Could Result In Potential Savings or Increased Revenues

Report title and number	Potential financial impact
Enhancing budget requests and implementing Patient Protection and Affordable Care Act (PPACA)	
IRS 2014 Budget: Improvements Made to Budget Request and Cost Estimate, but Further Actions Needed(GAO-13-835)	Increase Savings, Indirect Financial Benefit
IRS 2013 Budget: Continuing to Improve Information on Program Costs and Results Could Aid in Resource Decision Making(GAO-12-603)	Increase Savings, Indirect Financial Benefit
Enhancing electronic filing	
E-Filing Tax Returns: Penalty Authority and Digitizing More Paper Return Data Could Increase Benefits(GAO-12-33)	Increase Savings, Increase Savings and Revenue, Indirect Financial Benefit
Electronic Tax Return Filing: Improvements Can Be Made before Mandate Becomes Fully Implemented(GAO-11-344)	Increase Savings
Enhancing electronic filing and improving accuracy of paid preparers	
Tax Administration: Many Taxpayers Rely on Tax Software and IRS Needs to Assess Associated Risks(GAO-09-297)	Indirect Financial Benefit
Enhancing internal controls	

Table 9. (Continued)

Report title and number	Potential financial impact
Management Report: Improvements Are Needed to Enhance the Internal Revenue Service's Internal Controls(GAO-13-420R)	Increase Savings, Indirect Financial Benefit
Enhancing online taxpayer services	
IRS Website: Long-Term Strategy Needed to Improve Interactive Services(GAO-13-435)	Increase Savings, Indirect Financial Benefit
Enhancing private pension disclosures	
Private Pensions: Clarity of Required Reports and Disclosures Could Be Improved(GAO-14-92)	Indirect Financial Benefit
Enhancing taxpayer services	
2012 Tax Filing: IRS Faces Challenges Providing Service to Taxpayers and Could Collect Balances Due More Effectively(GAO-13-156)	Increase Savings and Revenue
2011 Tax Filing: Processing Gains, but Taxpayer Assistance Could Be Enhanced by More Self-Service Tools(GAO-12-176)	Increase Savings and Revenue
Enhancing treatment of appraisals issues	
Appraised Values on Tax Returns: Burdens on Taxpayers Could Be Reduced and Selected Practices Improved(GAO-12-608)	Increase Savings and Revenue
Enhancing verification of tax returns	
Tax Refunds: IRS Is Exploring Verification Improvements, but Needs to Better Manage Risks(GAO-13-515)	Indirect Financial Benefit
Expanding use of math error authority or third party data	
2011 Tax Filing: IRS Dealt with Challenges to Date but Needs Additional Authority to Verify year Compliance(GAO-11-481)	Increase Revenue
Recovery Act: IRS Quickly Implemented Tax Provisions, but Reporting and Enforcement Improvements Are Needed(GAO-10-349)	Increase Savings and Revenue
2009 Tax Filing Season: IRS Met Many 2009 Goals, but Telephone Access Remained Low, and Taxpayer Service and Enforcement Could Be Improved(GAO-10-225)	Increase Revenue, Increase Savings and Revenue
Tax Administration: IRS's 2008 Filing Season Generally Successful Despite Challenges, although IRS Could Expand Enforcement during Returns Processing(GAO-09-146)	Increase Savings and Revenue

Report title and number	Potential financial impact
Implementing Information Reporting and Document Matching (IRDM) system	
IRS Management: Cost Estimate for New Information Reporting System Needs to be Made More Reliable(GAO-12-59)	Indirect Financial Benefit
Information Reporting: IRS Could Improve Cost Basis and Transaction Settlement Reporting Implementation(GAO-11-557)	Indirect Financial Benefit
Implementing Patient Protection and Affordable Care Act (PPACA)	
Patient Protection and Affordable Care Act: IRS Should Expand Its Strategic Approach to Implementation(GAO-11-719)	Indirect Financial Benefit
Improving allocation of enforcement resources	
Tax Gap: IRS Could Significantly Increase Revenues by Better Targeting Enforcement Resources(GAO-13-151)	Increase Revenue
Improving administration of installment agreements	
2013 Tax Filing Season: IRS Needs to Do More to Address the Growing Imbalance between the Demand for Services and Resources(GAO-14-133)	Increase Savings
Improving collection of unpaid taxes from Medicaid providers	
Medicaid: Providers in Three States with Unpaid Federal Taxes Received Over $6 Billion in Medicaid Reimbursements(GAO-12-857)	Increase Savings
Improving corporate tax compliance	
Corporate Tax Compliance: IRS Should Determine Whether Its Streamlined Corporate Audit Process Is Meeting Its Goals(GAO-13-662)	Increase Revenue, Increase Savings, Indirect Financial Benefit
Tax Gap: Actions Needed to Address Noncompliance with S Corporation Tax Rules(GAO-10-195)	Increase Revenue
Improving examinations of tax returns	
Tax Administration: IRS Could Improve Examinations by Adopting Certain Research Program Practices(GAO-13-480)	Increase Revenue, Indirect Financial Benefit
Improving individual or corporate tax compliance	
Virtual Economies and Currencies: Additional IRS Guidance Could Reduce Tax Compliance Risks(GAO-13-516)	Increase Revenue
Federal Tax Collection: Potential for Using Passport Issuance to Increase Collection of Unpaid Taxes(GAO-11-272)	Increase Revenue

Table 9. (Continued)

Report title and number	Potential financial impact
Improving management of information technology (IT) investments	
Investment Management: IRS Has a Strong Oversight Process but Needs to Improve How It Continues Funding Ongoing Investments (GAO-11-587)	Increase Savings, Indirect Financial Benefit
Improving offshore compliance	
Offshore Tax Evasion: IRS Has Collected Billions of Dollars, But May be Missing Continued Evasion(GAO-13-318)	Increase Revenue, Indirect Financial Benefit
Improving real estate tax compliance	
Home Mortgage Interest Deduction: Despite Challenges Presented by Complex Tax Rules, IRS Could Enhance Enforcement and Guidance(GAO-09-769)	Increase Revenue
Improving rental real estate compliance	
Tax Gap: Actions That Could Improve Rental Real Estate Reporting Compliance(GAO-08-956)	Increase Revenue
Improving sole proprietors' compliance	
Tax Gap: Limiting Sole Proprietor Loss Deductions Could Improve Compliance but Would Also Limit Some Legitimate Losses(GAO-09-815)	Indirect Financial Benefit
Improving tax credit administration	
Small Employer Health Tax Credit: Factors Contributing to Low Use and Complexity(GAO-12-549)	Increase Savings and Revenue
Improving third party compliance	
Tax Gap: IRS Could Do More to Promote Compliance by Third Parties with Miscellaneous Income Reporting Requirements(GAO-09-238)	Increase Revenue, Indirect Financial Benefit
Improving use of whistleblower claims	
Tax Whistleblowers: Incomplete Data Hinders IRS's Ability to Manage Claim Processing Time and Enhance External Communication(GAO-11-683)	Increase Revenue
Promoting effective use of third-party data	
Tax Gap: IRS Has Modernized Its Business Nonfiler Program but Could Benefit from More Evaluation and Use of Third-Party Data(GAO-10-950)	Increase Revenue, Indirect Financial Benefit
Reducing tax evasion	
Tax Gap: IRS Can Improve Efforts to Address Tax Evasion by Networks of Businesses and Related Entities(GAO-10-968)	Indirect Financial Benefit

Source: GAO.

Notes: Products with open matters and recommendations identified as of March 13, 2014. Some products may have matters and/or recommendations that do not have potential financial benefits or could be placed in different categories than provided above.

APPENDIX III: COMMENTS FROM THE INTERNAL REVENUE SERVICE

DEPARTMENT OF THE TREASURY
INTERNAL REVENUE SERVICE
WASHINGTON, D.C. 20224

DEPUTY COMMISSIONER

June 3, 2014

Mr. James R. McTigue, Jr.
Director, Tax Issues
U.S. Government Accountability Office
441 G Street, N.W.
Washington, DC 20548

Dear Mr. McTigue:

Thank you for the opportunity to review the draft GAO report, IRS 2015 BUDGET: Long-term Strategy and Return on Investment Data Needed to Better Manage Budget Uncertainty and Set Priorities (GAO-14-605). We are pleased the GAO recognizes the significant funding reductions we have experienced since fiscal year 2010 and the impact those reductions have had on our staffing and performance as well as the steps that we have taken in recent years to reduce spending.

Below are the IRS's comments on each specific recommendation.

Recommendation #1: As a result of turnover in IRS's Senior Executive Team and in order to enhance budget planning and improve decision making and accountability, we recommend IRS:

- develop a long-term strategy to address operations amidst an uncertain budget environment. As part of the strategy, IRS should take steps to improve its efficiency including (1) reexamining programs, related processes, and organizational structures to determine whether it is effectively and efficiently achieving the mission and (2) streamlining or consolidating management or operational processes and functions to make them more cost-effective.

Comment: We agree with this recommendation. The IRS is currently conducting a review of the IRS budget base to ensure resources are aligned with IRS Strategic Goals, Objectives, and Priorities. The IRS base budget will be adjusted for FY 2015 with all permanent changes incorporated into the FY 2016 President's Budget due to Congress February 2015.

Recommendation #2: Because Return on Investment (ROI) provides insights on the productivity of a program and is one important factor in making resource allocation decisions, we recommend IRS:

- calculate actual ROI for implemented initiatives, compare the actual ROI to projected ROI, and provide the comparison to budget decision makers for initiatives where IRS allocated resources; and
- use actual ROI calculations as part of resource allocation decisions.

Comment: The IRS understands and recognizes the importance of having timely and relevant data to assist in understanding the effectiveness of its programs. We agree that ROI is one of several factors relevant to making resource allocation decisions. Other relevant factors include the use of cost/benefit, coverage, and balanced measures information in making resource allocation decisions.

The IRS further agrees that exploring ways to improve the estimates of benefits produced by new initiatives is worthwhile. However, determining the impact of an initiative will always rely on estimates, as the results of an initiative are the difference between actual results and what would have occurred in the absence of the initiative, which cannot be measured.

If you have any questions, please contact me, or a member of your staff may contact Adina Leach, Associate Chief Financial Officer for Corporate Budget, at (202) 317-6935.

Sincerely,

Peggy Sherry

Peggy Sherry
Deputy Commissioner for
Operations Support

End Notes

[1] GAO, Internal Revenue Service: Absorbing Budget Cuts Has Resulted in Significant Staffing Declines and Uneven Performance, GAO-14-534R (Washington, D.C.: Apr. 21, 2014).

[2] This report updates our interim report. As of April 19, 2014, after the completion of the filing season, fiscal year 2014 telephone level of service was 67 percent and wait time was 17.0 minutes.

[3] Pub. L. No. 111-148, 124 Stat. 119 (2010), as amended by the Health Care and Education Reconciliation Act of 2010 (HCERA), Pub. L. No. 111-152, 124 Stat. 1029, which we refer to collectively as PPACA. IRS refers to PPACA by the acronym for the Affordable Care Act, ACA.

[4] We will report on the September 2013 PPACA cost estimate once it is released for our review.

[5] See, for example, the Consolidated Appropriations Act, 2014, Pub. L. No. 113-76, div. E, title VI, § 608, 128 Stat. 5, 226 (Jan. 17, 2014). Reprogramming shifts funds within an appropriation account and, unlike transfers, agencies may reprogram without additional statutory authority; however, reprogramming above a statutorily defined threshold often

involves some form of notification to the congressional appropriations committees, authorizing committees, or both.

[6] Housing Assistance Tax Act of 2008, Pub. L. No. 110-289, div. C, §3091, 122 Stat. 2654, 2908-2911 (July 30, 2008).

[7] Energy Improvement and Extension Act of 2008, Pub. L. No. 110-343, div. B, §403, 122 Stat. 3765, 3854-3860 (Oct. 3, 2008).

[8] Hiring Incentives to Restore Employment Act, Pub. L. No. 111-147, Title V, 124 Stat. 71, 97-117 (Mar. 18, 2010).

[9] GAO-14-534R. This report focused on fiscal years 2009 through 2015. We selected fiscal year 2009 as a starting point because fiscal year 2009 was the year prior to IRS's highest appropriation in recent years.

[10] Sequestration is the reduction or cancellation of budgetary resources provided by discretionary appropriations or direct spending laws. Amounts are subject to sequestration under a presidential sequester order. On March 1, 2013, the President ordered a sequestration to achieve $85.3 billion in reductions across federal government accounts, as required by the Balanced Budget and Emergency Deficit Control Act of 1985, as amended. See 2 U.S.C. § 901a and Sequestration Order for Fiscal Year 2013 Pursuant to Section 251A of the Balanced Budget and Emergency Deficit Control Act, As Amended, 78 Fed. Reg. 14633 (Mar. 6, 2013).

[11] Consolidated Appropriations Act, 2014, Pub. L. No. 113-76, div. E, title I, 128 Stat. 5, 188-89, 190-91 (Jan. 17, 2014).

[12] From January 1 through April 19, 2014, the telephone level of service was 71 percent.

[13] The overage correspondence reported is for two IRS units that handle correspondence—Submission Processing and Accounts Management—both of which are part of W&I.

[14] See Internal Revenue Service Oversight Board, "Fiscal Year 2014 Budget Recommendation and Special Report, May 2013," National Taxpayer Advocate, 2013 Annual Report to Congress, Volume 1 (Dec. 31, 2013).

[15] The efforts described here do not include all of the savings and efficiencies listed in the fiscal year 2015 congressional justification for IRS.

[16] IRS reduced the number of furlough days to 3 days in part by exercising its authority to carry over roughly $52 million in unobligated funds from fiscal year 2012 appropriations.

[17] See GAO, 2012 Tax Filing: IRS Faces Challenges Providing Service to Taxpayers and Could Collect Balances Due More Effectively, GAO-13-156 (Washington, D.C.: Dec. 18, 2012).

[18] However, IRS officials note that it has allowed exceptions to the hiring freeze for high priority programs to help mitigate the impact of attrition in those areas.

[19] IRS's Senior Executive Team is comprised of its highest level members of the senior executive service, including the Commissioners, Deputy Commissioners, Chief Financial Officer, Office Directors, Chief Human Capital Officer, and Chief Counsel.

[20] IRS's budget was largely on an upward trajectory from fiscal year 2002 through fiscal year 2010.

[21] GAO, Fiscal Outlook: Federal Fiscal Outlook (Spring 2014), (Washington, D.C.: 2014), accessed on June 3, 2014, http://www.gao.gov/fiscal_outlook/federal_fiscal_outlook/overview.

[22] Specifically, OMB stated, "Unless your agency has been given explicit direction otherwise by OMB, your FY 2016 budget submission to OMB should reflect a 2 percent reduction below the net discretionary total provided for your agency for FY 2016 in the FY 2015 Budget, for each of the defense and nondefense discretionary categories." Office of Management and

Budget, Fiscal Year 2016 Budget Guidance, Memorandum M-14-07 (Washington, D.C.: May 5, 2014).

[23] The BCA imposed discretionary spending limits for fiscal years 2012 to 2021 to reduce projected spending by about $1 trillion. If the discretionary spending caps are not met in a given fiscal year, they will be enforced by an "after session sequestration" within 15 days after the end of a congressional session. Pub. L. No. 112-25, 125 Stat. 240 (Aug. 2, 2011).

[24] Executive Order No. 13576. Delivering an Efficient, Effective, and Accountable Government, 76 Fed. Reg. 35297 (June 16, 2011). In addition, a June 28, 2011 OMB memorandum outlined specific steps that CFOs should take to address the administration's directive to identify, execute, and report on administrative cost savings, including steps to identify and share best government practices that cut costs and improve efficiency. Office of Management and Budget, Campaign to Cut Waste (Washington, D.C.: June 28, 2011). See also Office of Management and Budget, Planning for Uncertainty with Respect to Fiscal Year 2013 Budgetary Resources, Memorandum M-13-03 (Washington, D.C.: Jan. 14, 2013) for guidance on preparing plans to operate within a reduced budgetary environment if sequestration occurs.

[25] GAO, Streamlining Government: Key Practices from Select Efficiency Initiatives Should Be Shared Governmentwide, GAO-11-908 (Washington, D.C.: Sept. 30, 2011).

[26] Key practices included (1) using change management practices to implement and sustain efficiency initiatives, (2) targeting both short-term and long-term efficiency initiatives, and (3) building capacity for improving efficiency. See GAO-11-908.

[27] GAO, IRS Website: Long-Term Strategy Needed to Improve Interactive Services, GAO-13-435 (Washington, D.C.: Apr. 16, 2013); GAO-13-156; Tax Gap: IRS Could Significantly Increase Revenues by Better Targeting Enforcement Resources, GAO-13-151 (Washington, D.C.: Dec. 5, 2012).

[28] IRS currently does not calculate ROI for taxpayer service initiatives.

[29] GAO, Internal Revenue Service: Review of the Fiscal Year 2010 Budget Request, GAO-09-754 (Washington, D.C.: June 3, 2009).

[30] Treasury Inspector General for Tax Administration, The Use of Return on Investment Information in Managing Tax Enforcement Resources Could be Improved, 2013-10-104 (Washington, D.C.: Sept. 23, 2013). In a February 2014 meeting with IRS, we discussed different approaches to calculating actual ROI. IRS officials told us they planned to take into consideration many factors and potential limitations to complete actual ROI calculations.

[31] GAO-09-754.

[32] Office of Management and Budget, Preparation and Submission of Strategic Plans, Annual Performance Plans, and Annual Program Performance Results, OMB Circular A11 (Washington, D.C.: June 2008); Office of Management and Budget, Guidelines and Discount Rates for Benefit-Cost Analysis of Federal Programs, OMB Circular A-94 (Washington, D.C.: undated); GAO, Tax Administration: IRS Needs to Further Refine Its Tax Filing Season Performance Measures, GAO-03-143 (Washington, D.C.: Nov. 22, 2002).

[33] GAO-09-754.

[34] A marginal ROI can be defined as the ratio of revenue generated from marginal enforcement cases, divided by the resources spent on working those cases. Marginal enforcement cases are those that would not have been worked if the resources allocated to a particular enforcement activity had been slightly less, as well as those additional cases that would have been worked if the resources for the activity had been slightly greater.

[35] GAO-13-151. In addition to indirect revenue effects through improved voluntary compliance, we also identified taxpayer compliance costs and effects on equity and economic efficiency as factors that are relevant but difficult to estimate. Taxpayers' perceived risks of being audited are recognized as a factor that influences voluntary compliance. The higher the risk of being audited, the less likely taxpayers are to evade taxes.

[36] If IRS's return selection process results in returns with the greatest revenue potential being worked first and those with the least potential being worked last, then each additional return that IRS examines with the expanded coverage would have a lower revenue yield than the average for all of the returns that had been examined up to that point. In other words, the marginal yield would be lower than the average yield.

[37] GAO-14-534R.

[38] GAO, GAO Cost Estimating and Assessment Guide: Best Practices for Developing and Managing Capital Program Costs, GAO-09-3SP (Washington, D.C.: Mar. 2, 2009).

End Notes for Appendix I

[1] Pub. L. No. 111-148, 124 Stat. 119 (2010), as amended by the Health Care and Education Reconciliation Act of 2010 (HCERA), Pub. L. No. 111-152, 124 Stat. 1029, which we refer to collectively as PPACA. IRS refers to PPACA by the acronym for the Affordable Care Act, ACA.

[2] We will report on the September 2013 PPACA cost estimate once it is released for our review.

INDEX

A

access, 8, 32, 33, 72
accessibility, 84
accountability, 39, 40, 87, 89
accounting, 54, 55
acquisitions, 2, 12
activity level, 7
adjustment, 48, 63, 64, 65, 66, 75, 76, 77, 91, 92
adjustment procedures, 48
advocacy, 7, 62
agencies, 13, 18, 35, 36, 53, 54, 58, 73, 74, 98
appraisals, 43, 94
appropriations, 1, 2, 5, 8, 9, 14, 64, 73, 99
Appropriations Act, 19, 98, 99
assessment, 23, 24, 25, 50, 89
assets, 19, 20, 64, 68, 79
audit(s), 6, 8, 17, 45, 48, 61, 67, 92
authority, 6, 8, 16, 43, 48, 49, 53, 54, 63, 94, 98, 99

B

bankruptcy, 12
banks, 64
base, 58, 73, 89, 90
benefits, 18, 26, 63, 90, 92, 93, 96
bias, 25
bonds, 64
breakdown, 50
budget cuts, vii, 2, 5, 11, 15, 57, 58, 60, 70, 71, 72, 73, 90, 91
budgetary resources, 53, 65, 66, 74, 99
business partners, 35
businesses, 12, 79

C

challenges, 77, 92
charitable organizations, 43
Chief of Staff, 16
clarity, 20
classification, 48
closure, 68
communication, 17
community, 12
compensation, 10
compliance, vii, 1, 3, 5, 7, 21, 26, 34, 41, 45, 46, 57, 58, 60, 65, 72, 75, 79, 89, 95, 96, 101
computer, 13, 34
computer technology, 34
Congress, 3, 6, 17, 18, 19, 20, 22, 26, 38, 47, 60, 62, 63, 65, 66, 78, 85, 86, 91, 92, 93, 99
congressional budget, 61, 79, 92
Consolidated Appropriations Act, 98, 99
coordination, 2, 5, 6, 16, 17

cost, 3, 6, 12, 13, 16, 18, 19, 21, 22, 23, 24, 25, 37, 39, 40, 49, 50, 51, 55, 60, 61, 63, 64, 66, 69, 72, 74, 75, 78, 83, 84, 85, 87, 88, 89, 90, 91, 92, 98, 100, 101
cost saving, 100
credit and debit card, 48
criminal investigations, 7
customer service, 63

D

data collection, 6, 61
decision makers, 37, 41, 78, 79, 81, 85, 89, 90
decision-making process, 17
deduction, 64
deficiencies, 17
Department of Health and Human Services, 81
Department of Justice, 12
Department of the Treasury, 36, 49, 63
deposits, 14
depreciation, 55
detection, 35, 62
direct cost, 79
diversity, 62
draft, 26, 90

E

Earned value management, 23
economic efficiency, 101
education, 7
employees, 13, 15, 22, 27, 32, 34, 35
employers, 22
employment, 13
enforcement, 21, 44, 45, 58, 62, 63, 73, 75, 77, 78, 79, 80, 81, 91, 95, 100
environment(s), vii, 1, 2, 40, 54, 58, 72, 73, 74, 75, 88, 89, 90, 100
equity, 62, 101
evidence, 6, 23, 25, 50, 51, 61, 73, 93
examinations, 45, 67, 79, 95
execution, 2, 5, 7, 16
executive order(s), 61, 74, 91, 100
exercise, 15

F

fairness, 5
federal government, vii, 1, 2, 4, 11, 18, 26, 53, 54, 57, 60, 99
financial, 3, 5, 17, 21, 33, 34, 42, 64, 92, 93, 94, 95, 96
financial institutions, 33
fires, 73
flexibility, 2, 8, 9, 14, 25, 48
fraud, 7, 33, 35, 46, 65, 69, 70, 72
funding, 6, 8, 9, 11, 13, 15, 28, 58, 60, 61, 62, 63, 64, 65, 66, 67, 72, 73, 75, 78, 81, 84, 88, 89, 90, 91, 92
funds, 7, 8, 9, 11, 14, 17, 22, 41, 53, 54, 62, 63, 71, 81, 98, 99

G

GAO, vii, 1, 2, 3, 6, 11, 14, 15, 21, 23, 24, 25, 26, 27, 28, 29, 30, 31, 36, 37, 38, 39, 40, 41, 42, 43, 44, 45, 46, 47, 48, 49, 51, 53, 54, 55, 57, 58, 59, 60, 65, 66, 68, 74, 77, 82, 83, 84, 85, 86, 87, 88, 91, 92, 93, 94, 95, 96, 98, 99, 100, 101
goods and services, 54
greed, 26, 87, 90
growth, 73
guidance, 2, 6, 12, 26, 36, 39, 54, 57, 58, 59, 61, 71, 74, 78, 86, 87, 91, 92, 100

H

health, 22, 27, 64, 73
Health and Human Services, 81
health care, 73
hiring, 15, 16, 25, 70, 72, 78, 84, 99
House, 4, 60
House of Representatives, 4, 60
human, 62
human resources, 62

I

identification, 17, 62, 63, 65, 72, 77
identity, 7, 35, 49, 64, 65, 69
image, 35
improvements, 63
income, 34, 62, 64, 67, 72
indirect effect, 58, 79
individual taxpayers, 79
individuals, 12, 33, 64, 78
industry, 12
inflation, 22, 27, 28, 49, 50, 53, 55
information technology, vii, 2, 4, 5, 12, 26, 38, 46, 60, 90, 96
infrastructure, 35
institutions, 33, 64
integrity, 5, 63, 64, 65, 66, 75, 76, 77, 91, 92
internal controls, 17, 26, 42, 93
Internal Revenue Service, vii, 2, 4, 42, 43, 52, 53, 58, 59, 60, 90, 93, 94, 97, 98, 99, 100
investment(s), vii, 1, 2, 3, 4, 5, 6, 8, 14, 17, 18, 19, 20, 21, 26, 32, 33, 34, 35, 36, 37, 38, 41, 46, 54, 58, 59, 60, 63, 64, 75, 84, 85, 86, 90, 96
IRS, vii, 1, 2, 3, 4, 5, 6, 7, 8, 9, 11, 12, 13, 14, 15, 16, 17, 18, 19, 20, 21, 22, 23, 24, 25, 26, 27, 28, 29, 30, 31, 32, 33, 34, 35, 36, 37, 38, 39, 40, 41, 42, 43, 44, 45, 46, 47, 48, 49, 51, 53, 54, 55, 57, 58, 59, 60, 61, 62, 63, 64, 65, 66, 67, 68, 69, 70, 71, 72, 73, 74, 75, 77, 78, 79, 80, 81, 82, 83, 84, 85, 86, 87, 88, 89, 90, 91, 92, 93, 94, 95, 96, 98, 99, 100, 101
issues, 12, 43, 63, 65, 72, 77, 94

J

justification, 2, 3, 5, 26, 27, 36, 47, 49, 57, 61, 62, 63, 67, 71, 72, 75, 77, 78, 79, 80, 84, 85, 91, 92, 99

L

laws, vii, 1, 12, 57, 60, 62, 64, 69, 89, 99
lead, 26
leadership, 58, 73, 75
legislative proposals, 5, 21
life cycle, 50
light, 89
litigation, 2, 7, 11, 12

M

magnitude, 71
majority, 11, 70, 73, 83
management, 8, 13, 14, 16, 18, 21, 23, 35, 39, 40, 45, 46, 50, 62, 72, 73, 74, 78, 87, 89, 96, 100
marginal costs, 41
materials, 85
matter, 92
Medicaid, 45, 95
Medicare, 48
methodology, 20, 50, 61
mission, 4, 8, 16, 17, 26, 40, 70, 74, 88, 89

N

negative effects, 79
negative outcomes, 26
nonenforcement, 37

O

Office of Management and Budget, 2, 4, 6, 55, 58, 59, 61, 91, 100
officials, 2, 6, 11, 12, 14, 15, 16, 18, 19, 20, 22, 23, 36, 37, 38, 58, 61, 67, 71, 72, 73, 77, 78, 79, 83, 87, 91, 92, 99, 100
OMB, 4, 6, 19, 26, 36, 54, 57, 58, 59, 61, 73, 74, 78, 84, 91, 92, 99, 100
operating system, 35
operations, 5, 14, 17, 18, 19, 40, 54, 61, 75, 88, 89, 90, 91

overhead costs, 15
oversight, 3, 18, 19, 43
overtime, 15, 16, 25
ownership, 33

P

payroll, 34, 70
penalties, 12, 49
pension plans, 62
platform, 35
policy, 54, 62
preparation, 17, 72
President, 1, 5, 6, 8, 13, 15, 57, 60, 65, 66, 67, 70, 84, 90, 91, 99
prevention, 65
procurement, 19
project, 78

Q

qualifications, 62

R

RAS, 59, 61
real estate, 46, 96
recommendations, vii, 1, 2, 3, 5, 6, 17, 21, 26, 42, 55, 58, 60, 61, 75, 83, 84, 85, 86, 87, 88, 90, 91, 92, 93, 96
Reform, 59, 81, 82
reforms, 64
regulations, 12, 13
regulatory changes, 22
reimburse, 13
reliability, 50
rent, 7, 62, 71
reparation, 100
requirements, 9, 12, 14, 15, 17, 22, 48, 49, 64, 72
resource allocation, 6, 17, 21, 40, 41, 58, 59, 79, 89, 90, 92
resources, 5, 8, 9, 14, 16, 22, 25, 28, 30, 37, 41, 44, 53, 58, 62, 63, 65, 66, 69, 73, 74, 75, 77, 79, 86, 89, 90, 95, 99, 100
response, 18, 21, 73
restrictions, 9, 16, 63
retirement, 47, 73
revenue, 2, 12, 13, 21, 25, 47, 49, 60, 62, 63, 75, 76, 77, 78, 79, 80, 91, 92, 93, 100, 101
risk(s), 2, 13, 15, 17, 18, 23, 26, 40, 51, 88, 101
ROI, vii, 4, 6, 21, 22, 41, 57, 58, 59, 60, 63, 75, 76, 77, 78, 79, 80, 81, 89, 90, 91, 100
rules, 24, 50

S

savings, 5, 47, 60, 70, 71, 85, 91, 92, 93, 99, 100
scope, 12, 22, 38, 61, 78, 79, 86
Secretary of the Treasury, 14
securities, 64
security, 7, 33, 62
Senate, 4, 60
sensitivity, 23, 39, 51, 83, 88
servers, 35
services, vii, 1, 2, 4, 7, 8, 13, 14, 25, 28, 30, 31, 33, 34, 35, 43, 54, 57, 60, 62, 67, 71, 72, 73, 75, 89, 94
software, 2, 12, 35
sole proprietor, 46, 96
solution, 72
specific tax, 81
spending, 2, 5, 9, 15, 16, 60, 61, 63, 65, 66, 70, 73, 81, 82, 88, 90, 91, 92, 99, 100
Spring, 99
staffing, vii, 1, 5, 23, 34, 60, 69, 91
stakeholders, 21, 85
states, 18
statistics, 62
statutes, 62
statutory authority, 8, 53, 63, 98
storage, 35
strategic planning, 17, 40, 62
structure, 7, 50, 54, 75, 88

T

target, 67
tax credits, 64
tax deduction, 64
tax evasion, 47, 96
tax system, 12, 25
taxes, vii, 1, 7, 8, 12, 45, 57, 60, 64, 79, 95, 101
taxpayers, 1, 4, 5, 8, 11, 12, 14, 16, 33, 34, 35, 36, 48, 57, 60, 67, 71, 75, 79, 89, 101
technical comments, 27, 90
techniques, 89
technology, vii, 2, 4, 5, 12, 26, 34, 38, 46, 60, 71, 72, 77, 90, 96
telecommunications, 8
telecommunications services, 8
telephone, 16, 34, 60, 67, 71, 72, 98, 99
theft, 7, 35, 49, 65, 69
time frame, 14
Title V, 99
tracks, 7
trade, 17, 37
trade-off, 17, 37
training, 16, 58, 70
trajectory, 99
transactions, 64
transparency, 17, 26, 84
Treasury, 14, 36, 48, 49, 54, 59, 63, 77, 91, 100
treatment, 43, 63, 77, 94
tuition, 47
turnover, 58, 73, 75, 89

U

uninsured, 64
United States, vii, 1, 4, 12, 54, 57, 60, 64
updating, 83, 92

W

Washington, 49, 53, 54, 55, 88, 92, 98, 99, 100, 101
web, 33, 35
workflow, 16
workforce, 69, 84
workload, 57, 69, 91

Y

yield, 101